A SWEDENBORG
PERPETUAL CALENDAR

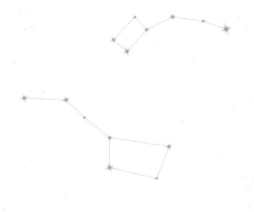

Em - Swedenborg.

A SWEDENBORG
PERPETUAL CALENDAR

Thoughts for the Day to Return to Year after Year

Text by Emanuel Swedenborg

Passages selected and arranged by Chelsea Rose Odhner

**SWEDENBORG
FOUNDATION**
West Chester, Pennsylvania

The present volume was inspired by and adapted from the 1902 edition of *A Swedenborg Perpetual Calendar* by Julia A. Kellogg. All of the passages within were taken from New Century Edition translations of the theological works of Emanuel Swedenborg, some of which have yet to be published. All passages used with permission.

The Library of Congress Cataloging-in-Publication Data is available upon request.
Library of Congress Control Number: 2023025173
ISBN-13: 978-0-87785-424-1 / e-ISBN-13: 978-0-87785-715-0

Design and typesetting by Karen Connor
Printed in the United States of America

Swedenborg Foundation
320 North Church Street
West Chester, PA 19380
www.swedenborg.com

CONTENTS

INTRODUCTION

WE INVITE YOU to take a contemplative journey, immersing yourself in these carefully selected passages from the New Century Edition translations of Emanuel Swedenborg's theological works. Each month is devoted to a theme, and each day shares an idea that expands upon and refines its month's topic. Altogether, what you now hold in your hands is a panoramic survey of Swedenborg's teachings that can support you wherever you are on your life's journey.

According to Swedenborg, meditating on the ideas found in these passages will stir the connection that each of us has to angels in heaven and to the source of divine love and wisdom, with your inner self acting as the conduit. By letting the ideas in this book infuse your consciousness, a whole host of questions will naturally emerge. For example, you might ask,

☽ "What is being awakened in me?"

☽ "What reactions, if any, do I feel arising in me?"

Introduction

- ❦ "Am I experiencing any particular emotions at this moment?"
- ❦ "Is my body responding to the words in a certain way?"
- ❦ "Are these ideas having an effect on my breathing?"
- ❦ "How does it feel in my heart?"
- ❦ "What sorts of deeper questions do these passages evoke in me?"

By picking up this book and considering the meaning behind its words, you are opening yourself up to the possibility of transformation, healing, and empowerment, thereby giving yourself the tools you need to be of use to the global community in a way in which only you can.

May the words on these pages serve your highest good and fill you with hope; may they bless your journey and inspire your imagination; may they allow you to sense your innate connection to heaven.

A NOTE ON
LANGUAGE FOR THE DIVINE

EMANUEL SWEDENBORG (1688–1772) wrote from, and lived within, a Christian framework, even though the substance of his theology expands beyond religious distinctions and so has an enduring universal appeal. Swedenborg often refers to the Divine as "the Lord," which is shorthand for "the Lord God Jesus Christ." While we are mindful of the apparent limiting nature of this term, and of the use of the masculine pronouns that it demands, we have maintained using both in this context to remain faithful to the original.

A SWEDENBORG
PERPETUAL CALENDAR

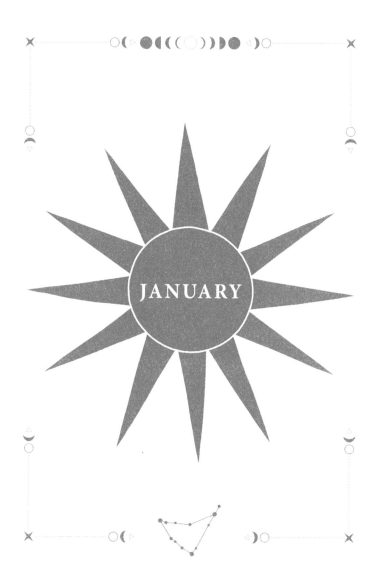

JANUARY

1 Infinite divinity cannot be described as anything but goodness and truth itself.

    —*Secrets of Heaven* 2011

2 Two things constitute the essence of God: divine love and divine wisdom; or, what is the same, divine goodness and divine truth.

    —*True Christianity* 85:2

3 The Infinite itself, which is high above all the heavens and high above our inmost reaches, cannot be revealed except through divine humanity, which exists only in the Lord.

    —*Secrets of Heaven* 1990:2

4 Divine truth is the same as divine humanity.

    —*Secrets of Heaven* 2643

5 In the Divine-Human One, reality and its manifestation are both distinguishable and united. These two are one entity in such a way that although they can be distinguished in thought they cannot be distinguished in fact; and since they can be distinguished in thought and not in fact, we refer to them as "distinguishably one." Reality and its manifestation are also distinguishably one in the

Divine-Human One the way soul and body are. A soul does not occur without its body, nor a body without its soul. The divine soul of the Divine-Human One is what we mean by the divine reality, and the divine body of the Divine-Human One is what we mean by the divine manifestation. The notion that a soul can exist and think and be wise without a body is an error that stems from deceptive appearances. Every soul is in a spiritual body after it has cast off the material skin that it carried around in this world.

—*Divine Love and Wisdom* 14

6 Nothing that is essential in an absolute sense exists anywhere in creation, only in the Supreme Being, that is, in the Lord.

—*Secrets of Heaven* 5948:3

7 When we love what is good, we love the Lord, because the Lord is the source of goodness, the presence within goodness, and identical with goodness itself.

—*Secrets of Heaven* 6818

8 There is only one life, the Lord's life, which flows into everyone. But we receive that life in various ways, according to

the character we have stamped on our soul by the way we lived in the world. Note that life from the Lord is a life of love for the entire human race.

—*Secrets of Heaven* 6467

9 It is because the very essence of the Divine is love and wisdom that we have two abilities of life. From the one we get our discernment, and from the other volition. Our discernment is supplied entirely by an inflow of wisdom from God, while our volition is supplied entirely by an inflow of love from God.

—*Divine Love and Wisdom* 30

10 The inner self in us lies above our rational mind and is the Lord's.

—*Secrets of Heaven* 2093:4

11 There is only one life force, which is the Lord's, and it flows in and causes us to live—both those of us who are good and those of us who are evil.

—*Secrets of Heaven* 3001

12 One of the most important kinds of intelligence angels have is to know and perceive that all life comes from the

Lord, that heaven as a whole corresponds to his divine humanity, and consequently that all angels, spirits, and people correspond to heaven. It is also to know and perceive how they correspond. These are the fundamentals of the intelligence in which angels excel, compared to us. It enables them to have immeasurable knowledge and perception about the heavens and therefore about the world, since the phenomena of the world and nature are means and results flowing from heavenly phenomena as their origins. The whole material world is a theater representing the Lord's kingdom.

—*Secrets of Heaven* 4318

13 Even though the word "love" is so commonly on our tongues, still hardly anyone knows what love is. We are wholly unaware that it is our very life—not just the general life of our whole body and of all our thoughts, but the life of their every least detail.

—*Divine Love and Wisdom* 1

14 People do their thinking based on some love. Take away the love: can they think anything at all? It is exactly the same as taking the sound out of speech. If you take away the sound, can you say anything at all? In fact, sound comes from a desire related to some love, and speech comes from thought, since love makes the sound, and thought speaks.

—*True Christianity* 388:6

15 Goodness and truth resemble babies, in that they are conceived, grow in the womb, are born, grow up, and increase in age until they reach full maturity. Conception, gestation, and birth belong to their rise; growing up and aging till they reach full maturity belong to their progress. The stage of progress, in which goodness and truth unite, follows birth, and its start is what *growing up* symbolizes. This stage begins right after birth and continues all the way to the end of life, and in people devoted to goodness, it continues beyond bodily life to eternity. In other words, angels are always developing.

—*Secrets of Heaven* 3308

16 Evil and sin viewed in themselves are nothing but a rift with goodness. Evil actually consists in disconnection.

—*Secrets of Heaven* 4997

17 We were created to have an intellect and will that compose a single mind, which is what happens when our intellect is at one with our will—that is, when our thoughts and words match our intent and deeds. Then the contents of our intellect are forms manifesting our will. The contents of the intellect are what are called truths, because truth belongs to the intellect. The contents of the will are what are called goodness, because goodness belongs to the will. It follows, then, that regarded in itself, any product of the intellect is simply a product of the will given shape.

—*Secrets of Heaven* 4574:2

18 Our genuine will is our inmost core, because it forms out of our love. Whatever we love, we will, and what we love most of all, we will the most deeply. Our intellect, on the other hand, [merely] serves to reveal to others what we will, or what we love.

—*Secrets of Heaven* 8885:3

19 It is willing that makes a person human, and not so much knowing and understanding.

—*Secrets of Heaven* 585

20 Our spirits are our minds and whatever comes from them. Our "spirit" really means nothing else but our mind.

—*True Christianity* 156

On the inside the human mind is constructed of spiritual substances, and on the outside, of earthly substances and finally physical materials.

—*True Christianity* 38:3

21 Every person born has an inner part; our outer part is the means by which we actually do what faith and love (and consequently our inner part) urge us to do. The inner part is what is called the soul, and the outer part is what is called the body.

—*Secrets of Heaven* 10592

22 Our earthly self, as it relates to our reasoning self (or our outward self as it relates to our inward) resembles the manager of a household. Everything in us works the way a single household does, or in other words, the way a single family does. There is the part that functions as the head of the household and the parts that function as servants. The rational mind itself is what oversees everything as the head of the household and organizes the earthly mind by exerting an influence on it. The earthly mind is what carries out and administers orders. The earthly mind is distinct from the reasoning mind and occupies a lower level but also acts with some autonomy.

—*Secrets of Heaven* 3020:1–2

23 A moral life may be lived either to satisfy the Divine or to satisfy people in this world. A moral life that is lived to satisfy the Divine is a spiritual life.

—*Heaven and Hell* 319

24 The Lord's foresight and providence concerns itself with the smallest possible aspects in human affairs—so small that we cannot in any way comprehend one out of millions. Every split second of our life carries with it a series of consequences that continues forever. Each moment is like a new starting point for another series, and this is true for each and every moment of life in both our intellect and our will. Since the Lord foresaw from eternity what we would be like now and forever, his providence must obviously be present in the smallest facets, governing us and (again) bending us in this direction by continually moderating our freedom.

—*Secrets of Heaven* 3854:3

25 It is when we are being reborn, as adults who possess knowledge, that goodness comes out into the open. Then we want not so much to know truth as to act on it. Up to that point, truth existed in the intellect, but afterward it exists in the will, and when it exists in the will, it exists in the person—since the will constitutes a person's real self.

Such is the ever-repeating cycle in a person: every form of secular and religious knowledge enters through our eyes or ears into our thoughts, from there into our will, and from there through our thoughts into act. The starting point can also be the memory, which resembles inner sight, or the inner eye. A similar cycle begins there, moving from the inner eye through the thoughts into the will and from the will through the thoughts into action. If anything blocks it, the cycle ends in the effort to act, which proceeds to action as soon as the blockage is removed.

—*Secrets of Heaven* 4247:2

26 It needs to be known that our spirit is in our body, in the whole and in every part of it. It is our purer substance, in both our motor and our sensory organs and everywhere else. Our body is the matter attached to it at every point and suited to the world in which we now are. That is what I mean by saying that a human being is a spirit, that the body serves as a tool for useful activity in the world, that the spirit is our inner part, and that the body is our outer part. These comments also show that after death we have a similar life of action and sensation, and that we are in a human shape as in the world, but a more perfect one.

—*Secrets of Heaven* 4659

27 It is the spirit within us that thinks, and thought and affection together make us the people we are.

   —Heaven and Hell 445

28 We should all look out for our body by providing it with food and clothing. This has to come first, but the goal must be a healthy mind in a healthy body. And we should also look out for our mind by providing it with food— that is, with ideas that nourish understanding and wisdom—so that it will be in a position to serve the Lord. If we do this, we take good eternal care of ourselves.

   —Secrets of Heaven 6936

29 In heaven, morning is a state of enlightenment regarding questions of goodness and truth. This state comes into being when we acknowledge, and particularly when we perceive, that goodness is good and truth true. Perception is inner revelation, so morning symbolizes what is revealed. Since what was formerly obscure then becomes clear, morning also symbolizes clarity.

   —Secrets of Heaven 5097

30 All revelation comes either from dialog with angels through whom the Lord speaks or from perception.

   —Secrets of Heaven 5121

31 People intent on goodness and therefore on truth—and especially on the goodness that comes from loving the Lord—have revelation from perception. People not intent on goodness and therefore on truth can have revelation but not from perception, only through a living voice they hear inside them, that is, through angels from the Lord. Audible revelation is outward; revelation from perception is inward.

—*Secrets of Heaven* 5121:2

FEBRUARY

1 We are one with spirits and angels. In fact, we ourselves are spirits clothed in flesh.

—*Secrets of Heaven* 69

2 It is essentially human and therefore angelic to base our thoughts on the truth; and the truth is that we do not think on our own but that the Lord enables us to think, to all appearances autonomously.

—*Divine Providence* 321:5

3 The divine design is that we arrange ourselves for receiving God and prepare ourselves as a vessel and a dwelling place where God can enter and live as if we were his own temple. We have to do this preparation by ourselves, yet we have to acknowledge that the preparation comes from God. This acknowledgment is needed because we do not feel the presence or the actions of God, even though God is in fact intimately present and brings about every good love and every true belief we have.

—*True Christianity* 105

4 Sights seen in the threefold kingdom of the physical world are the outermost elements of the divine design,

because they form a perimeter for all the elements of
heaven, which are called spiritual and heavenly.

—*Secrets of Heaven* 10728

5 Heaven's union with us is not like the union of one person
with another, but is a union with the deeper levels of our
minds and therefore with our spiritual or inner person.

—*Heaven and Hell* 300

6 Knowing about levels is a kind of key to unlocking the
causes of things and probing into them. "Gradual levels"
is the name we give to declines or decreases from coarser
to finer or denser to rarer, or better, to gains or increases
from finer to coarser or from rarer to denser. They are
just like going from light to darkness or from warmth to
cold. In contrast, distinct levels are totally different. They
are like antecedent, subsequent, and final events, or like
the purpose, the means, and the result.

—*Divine Love and Wisdom* 184

7 For angels, these three levels are called heavenly, spiritual, and earthly; and for them, the heavenly level is the
level of love, the spiritual level the level of wisdom, and
the earthly level the level of useful functions.

—*Divine Love and Wisdom* 232

8 True humanity consists of rationality (which is the same as the inner self) and earthliness (the outer self). It also includes the body, which serves the earthly level as a means or outermost organ for living in the world. Through the earthly level it serves the rational level, and through this, the divine level.

—*Secrets of Heaven* 3737

9 In us we have vital energy on the sensory level and vital energy on the earthly level, both kinds of energy being located in our outer self. The sensory-level energy is relatively shallow and draws its truths from objects in the physical world and in our body, while the earthly-level energy is deeper and draws its truths from the causes that bring those objects into being.

—*Secrets of Heaven* 10254

10 Hardly anyone today knows what the outer self is, because people think that everything making up the outer self is connected with the body, such as its senses (touch, taste, smell, hearing, and sight), appetites, and pleasures. These constitute the most external self, however, which is purely physical.

—*Secrets of Heaven* 1718

11 The divine plan is for the Lord to influence our outer levels through our inner levels and consequently our actions through our will.

—*Secrets of Heaven* 8513:2

12 A word about heavenliness and spirituality: Heavenliness itself and spirituality itself, which flow into heaven from the Lord's divinity, reside mainly on our inner rational plane, the forms that exist on that plane being more perfect and suited to receiving the inflow. However, heavenliness and spirituality also flow from the Lord's divinity into our outer rational plane, and into our earthly plane as well. What is more, they flow in both indirectly and directly—indirectly through the inner rational dimension, and directly from the Lord's divinity itself. What flows in directly is an organizing force, and what flows in indirectly is what is organized.

—*Secrets of Heaven* 5150

13 There are several levels (like steps on a ladder) between the intellect and the senses, but no one can begin to understand them without knowing something about them and the fact that the different levels are utterly distinct from each other. In fact, they are so distinct that the inner levels can emerge into lasting existence without the outer levels, although the outer levels cannot do so without the inner. For instance, our spirit can exist without our body and its matter, and does exist without them when separated from the body by death. Our spirit is on an inner plane and our body on an outer one.

The same thing happens with our spirit after death, if we are among the blessed. We are on the lowest level there when we are in the first heaven, on an inner level when we are in the second, and on the inmost level when we are in the third. When we are in the third heaven, we are actually in the others too, but these other levels are unconscious in us, in almost the same way that our body is unconscious during sleep. The difference is that in heaven our inner levels are wide awake among the angels. There are as many distinctly different levels in us, then, as there are heavens, except for the last level, which is the body with its senses.

—*Secrets of Heaven* 5114:3

14 Our soul is one with our body; our inner core is one with our outer shell, even though they are distinct from one another. Sometimes the distinction between them is so great that one fights the other, as commonly happens in times of trial. At those times, our inner core upbraids our outer shell and tries to get rid of the evil in our outer shell, and yet they are closely connected or form a single whole, because both soul and body belong to the same person.

—*Secrets of Heaven* 2018

15 Our inner dimension comes to life in our outer dimension through what we actually do. If what we do does not conform to what is inside us, it indicates one of two things. Either it does not come from something internal but instead is a motion we repeat by custom and habit, or it is a sham like that of hypocrisy or deceit.

—*Secrets of Heaven* 3934:3

16 If the outer self is to be reduced to order, it must become subordinate to the inner self, and it does not become subordinate until it becomes obedient. The more obedient and subordinate the outer self becomes, the wiser it also becomes.

—*Secrets of Heaven* 9708

17 When the spiritual mind is open, the state of the earthly mind is entirely different. Then the earthly mind is inclined to obey the spiritual mind and be subservient.

—*Divine Love and Wisdom* 263

18 When we undergo inner challenges—that is, when our inner self undergoes challenges—the earthly level acts as a midwife. Unless the earthly level helps, no birth of inner truth ever takes place. The earthly level is what takes inner truth into its arms upon birth, since it gives truth the opportunity to make its way out. That is how the case stands with the offspring of spiritual birth; the earthly plane absolutely must be there to catch them. This is the reason that the first step in a person's regeneration is preparation of the earthly plane for reception; and the more receptive it grows, the greater the possibility for inner truth and goodness to be brought forth and multiply.

—*Secrets of Heaven* 4588

19 We acquire justice the more we practice it. We practice justice the more our interaction with our neighbor is motivated by a love for justice and truth. Justice dwells in the goodness itself or the useful functions themselves that we do.

—*True Christianity* 96

20 A desire for facts is the mother that gives birth to the kind of rationality that has a spiritual core.

—*Secrets of Heaven* 2675

21 When we are engaged in earthly love and spiritual love together, then we are rational people.

    —*Divine Love and Wisdom* 416

22 Good on the earthly level is everything connected with earthly emotion, called pleasure. Truth there is everything qualifying as secular knowledge, called fact. The earthly dimension must embrace both if it is to be itself. Facts by themselves, without the pleasure that forms our emotional response to them, are nothing. The earthly level receives its life from earthly delight, since only delight makes it possible for us to learn anything. The pleasure that constitutes good on the earthly level is something without facts but not anything more than a liveliness of the kind seen in children. If the earthly dimension is to be human, then, it must consist of both; the one entity is complemented by the other. It receives its life, though, from goodness.

    —*Secrets of Heaven* 3293

23 The earthly goodness that we acquire (or that the Lord gives us as a gift) has a spiritual impulse in it, so that spiritual goodness is within the earthly. This goodness is the real earthly, human kind.

    —*Secrets of Heaven* 3408

24 Since the deeper levels present themselves together on the outermost level, then, the outermost level (as I said) is considered holier than the inner levels (provided the entire pattern is complete) because the holiness of the inner depths finds its fulfillment there.

—*Secrets of Heaven* 9824:3

25 There are always two forces that keep everything connected and hold it together, one acting on the outside, and one on the inside. Between them is the object being maintained. There absolutely have to be two forces for anything to emerge and survive. There are earthly forces working on the outside that are not intrinsically alive and forces working on the inside, intrinsically alive, that hold everything together and enable it to live, in accordance with the form given to it for its function.

—*Secrets of Heaven* 3628:2, 3

26 We prepare ourselves to receive God and to forge a partnership with him by following the divine design in our lives. The laws of that design are all God's commandments.

—*True Christianity* 110:5

27 Our voluntary activity is always leading us away from the divine design, but our involuntary activity is always leading us back to it. That is why the motion of the heart, which is involuntary, is completely outside the province of human will, as is the action of the cerebellum. It is also why the motion of the heart and the forces of the cerebellum control voluntary action, to keep it from rushing beyond certain bounds and snuffing out the life of the body before its time.

—*Secrets of Heaven* 9683:2

28 We can tell that divine love is in all of us, the evil and the good alike, and that therefore the Lord who is divine love must treat us with as much love as an earthly father treats his children—with infinitely more love, in fact, because divine love is infinite. Further, he can never withdraw from anyone, because everyone's life comes from him.

—*Divine Providence* 330:2

29 No one can be united to the Lord except through love and charity. Love is spiritual union itself, as the very nature of love shows.

—*Secrets of Heaven* 2349:2

MARCH

1 In everything created there is some image of the divine love and wisdom that are a whole in the Lord and that emanate from him as a whole. This is why everything in the universe is based on what is good and what is true and in fact on their union, or (which amounts to the same thing) everything in the universe is based on love and wisdom and on their union, since goodness is a matter of love and truth is a matter of wisdom. Love in fact calls everything of its own good, and wisdom calls everything of its own true.

—*Divine Providence* 5:1, 2

2 Overall, the human mind has nothing else to focus on besides matters of truth and goodness. Its intellect focuses on matters of truth, and its will on matters of goodness.

—*Secrets of Heaven* 4390:2

3 There is a union of love and wisdom in every divine work. This is why it endures, even to eternity. If there were more divine love than divine wisdom or more divine wisdom than divine love in any created work, nothing would endure in it except what was equal. Any excess would pass away.

—*Divine Love and Wisdom* 36

4 Truth can come from anyone, but truth that is good can come only from the Lord.

—*Secrets of Heaven* 8301

5 We are all born human, which means that we have the image of God within us. The image of God within us is our ability to discern what is true and to do what is good. Our ability to discern what is true comes from divine wisdom and our ability to do what is good comes from divine love. This ability is the image of God; it is enduring with everyone who is whole and is never erased.

—*Divine Providence* 322

6 All goodness has its related truth, and all truth has its related goodness. Goodness without truth is invisible, and truth without goodness has no existence. Truth is the tangible form of goodness, and goodness is the vital essence of truth. From the tangible form, goodness acquires visibility, and from the vital essence, truth acquires its existence.

—*Secrets of Heaven* 9637

7 In order to exist, everything good or true must be within something for which it forms the underlying substance.

Goodness and truth cannot exist as abstractions, since if they did they would have nothing in which to reside and could not be even fleetingly visualized.

—*Marriage Love* 66

8 Goodness flows in along an inner route unknown to us, but truth is acquired by an outer route that we know about.

—*Secrets of Heaven* 3324:3

9 What is good contains the Lord, you see, and consequently contains heaven, so it contains life and therefore a living, driving force. Truth lacking in goodness contains none of this force.

—*Secrets of Heaven* 5704

10 Truth is what power is attributed to, because goodness works through truth when wielding power.

—*Secrets of Heaven* 4402:5

That is why goodness has potential but a potential that is not focused on an object except through truth.

—*Secrets of Heaven* 9643

11 All God's strength, force, and power belong to the divine truth that comes from divine goodness.
—*True Christianity* 86

12 Unless it is married to wisdom, love cannot accomplish anything.
—*Divine Providence* 4

13 Truth is introduced and united to goodness when we love God and love our neighbor, because truth then takes up residence in goodness, since goodness and truth acknowledge one another. All truth comes from goodness, and truth looks to goodness as its ultimate aim and its soul and so as the source of its life.
—*Secrets of Heaven* 3175:2

14 No one can know what is good without also knowing what is not good, and no one can know what is true without knowing what is not true.
—*Secrets of Heaven* 5356:2

15 To possess goodness and truth is not merely to know them, or hold them in our memory and carry them on our lips, but to respond to them from the heart. Nor are they ours when we seek them for the sake of amassing prestige and wealth. In that case it is not goodness and truth we seek but position and riches; we view goodness and truth as the means of acquiring them.

—*Secrets of Heaven* 3402:3

16 All spiritual purification is brought about by truth. We do not recognize the earthly and worldly types of love from which we need to be purified except through truth.

—*Secrets of Heaven* 7918

17 The truth in us can never be purified of falsity without virtual leavening, or so-called fermentation—that is, without a fight put up by falsity against truth and by truth against falsity. After the fight is finished and truth has conquered, falsity drops away like the waste products of fermentation, and truth stands purified, like wine, which clarifies upon fermentation, the dregs settling to the bottom.

—*Secrets of Heaven* 7906:2

18 As soon as goodness takes control in us, our earthly, outer self surrenders and we become a spiritual church. The validity of this statement can be recognized from the fact that inclination then leads us to do what truth teaches us to do; we do not violate that inclination, no matter how intensely our earthly plane wants us to. Genuine desire and consequent rationality rule us, subduing the pleasures of self-love and materialism present on our earthly plane, as well as the illusions that have permeated the facts stored there. The conquest is eventually so complete that we count it as one of our greater satisfactions, at which point our earthly dimension quiets down and then comes into harmony. When it comes into harmony, it shares the inner dimension's sense of satisfaction.

—*Secrets of Heaven* 6567:1–2

19 Love or volition does not do anything without wisdom or discernment. Since love has neither sensory nor active life apart from discernment, and since love leads discernment into all the functions of the mind, it follows that love or volition does not do anything apart from discernment. What would it be to act from love apart from discernment? We could only call it something senseless. Discernment is what shows us what needs to be done and how it needs to be done. Love does not know this apart from discernment.

—*Divine Love and Wisdom* 409

20 In all unions there is action and reaction. The active force is goodness, and the reactive force is truth. Yet truth never reacts on its own, only under the power of goodness.

—*Secrets of Heaven* 10729:2

21 Sometimes things look evil even when they do not well up and flow out from evil within, from an evil intention or aim, but they are not evil if the aim is not.

—*Secrets of Heaven* 4839

22 Absolutely everyone in the heavens and on earth has a different sort of goodness. One and the same kind of goodness can never exist in two people; it has to vary in order for each kind to remain in existence separately.

—*Secrets of Heaven* 6706

23 True religious concepts are the actual vessels that receive goodness, and they receive goodness so far as we move away from evil. What is good is always streaming into us from the Lord, but what is evil in our lives keeps it from being received in the truth we memorize or know. So the more we back away from evil, the more goodness enters into us and adapts to the truth we have.

—*Secrets of Heaven* 2388:2

24 The goodness in us does not become spiritual until it has been given form by truth.

—*Secrets of Heaven* 8889

25 Neighborly love is a deep emotional response that consists in this: that we sincerely want to do good to our neighbor, that this is our highest pleasure, and that we want to do it without being repaid.

—*Secrets of Heaven* 8033

26 Faith is a deep emotional response that consists in this: that we sincerely want to know what is true and good, not for the sake of theology as our ultimate goal but rather for the sake of our life.

—*Secrets of Heaven* 8034

27 A life of faith consists in following the Commandments out of obedience, and a life of neighborly love in following them out of love.

—*Secrets of Heaven* 9193:3

28 Charitable deeds consist in our doing what is just and fair, each of us in our own job, from a love of justice and fairness and of goodness and truth.

—*Secrets of Heaven* 4783:5

29 The reward for people who have neighborly love is the ability and opportunity to do good and the reception of the good they do.

—*Secrets of Heaven* 3956

30 Ability is assigned to truth, whereas beingness is assigned to goodness. Goodness acquires power through truth, because it is through truth that goodness drives everything that happens.

—*Secrets of Heaven* 3910

31 The goodness of love and the truth of faith are more than abstractions devoid of the power to make anything happen. In reality the opposite is true: all perception and sensation, all force and action rise out of love's goodness and faith's truth, even in people on earth.

—*Secrets of Heaven* 3887:2

APRIL

1 Something that appears like a soul and a body exists in every facet of our being—in every facet of our feelings and in every facet of our thinking.

—*Secrets of Heaven* 1910

2 Everything that happens in the physical world is an effect and everything that happens in the spiritual world is a cause of such effects. Nothing happens in nature that does not have its cause in the spiritual realm.

—*Divine Love and Wisdom* 134

3 Intellect and volition are our spiritual person.

—*Heaven and Hell* 228

4 We have two faculties for receiving life from the Lord. One is called will, and the other, intellect. These two faculties must constitute a single mind if we are to be truly human.

—*Secrets of Heaven* 9050:1, 6

5 The life of the will always comes first and the life of the intellect second.

—*Secrets of Heaven* 5969

6 People find it hard to distinguish between thought and will. When we want something, we say we think it, and when we think something, we often say we want it. Yet the two differ the way truth and goodness do.

—*Secrets of Heaven* 9995:2

The intellectual side influences the will side when truth turns into goodness. The will side influences the intellectual side when it puts this truth-turned-goodness into practice.

—*Secrets of Heaven* 5077:4

7 We need to realize that we are all our own will and our own intellect. This is how one person is differentiated from another.

—*True Christianity* 263

From all this three points emerge: that our life finds its home in our intellect; that that life is only as good as our wisdom; and that that life is modified by the love in our will.

—*True Christianity* 39

Will and Intellect

8 The desire for good (doing good because you love good) is really a matter of will. The desire for truth, though, (doing good because you love truth) is really a matter of intellect. At first glance, these two kinds of desire look as though they were the same, but they are inherently different, both in essence and in origin.

—*Secrets of Heaven* 1997

9 Our life is found in its primary forms in our brains and in secondary forms in our bodies. "In its primary forms" means in its beginnings, and "in secondary forms" means in the things that are produced and formed from these beginnings. "Life in its primary forms" means volition and discernment. It is these two functions that occur in their primary forms in our brains and in their derivative forms in our bodies.

—*Divine Love and Wisdom* 365

10 The human cerebrum serves the intellect and its wisdom, whereas the cerebellum serves the will and its love.

—*True Christianity* 564:3

11 Anything that we have justified both volitionally and intellectually lasts forever, but not what we have justified only intellectually. Anything that is only in our discernment is not within us but outside us. It is only in our thought, and nothing really comes into us and becomes part of us except what is welcomed by our volition. This becomes part of our life's love.

—*Divine Providence* 318:11

12 If our intellect were incapable of being perfected on its own and of then perfecting our will, we would not be human at all; we would be animals. If there were no separation between our will and our intellect and if the intellect could not rise above the will, we would be unable either to think or to say what we thought. We would only be able to make noises that expressed our feelings.

—*True Christianity* 588:2

13 There are two abilities within us, gifts from the Lord, that distinguish us from animals. One ability is that we can discern what is true and what is good. This ability is called "rationality," and is an ability of our discernment. The other ability is that we can do what is true and what is good. This ability is called "freedom," and is an ability of our volition. The Lord lives in each of us, in the good and the evil alike, in these two abilities. They are the Lord's dwelling in the human race, which is why everyone, whether good or evil, lives forever. However, the Lord's dwelling within us is more intimate as we use these abilities to open the higher levels. By opening them, we come into consciousness of higher levels of love and wisdom and so come closer to the Lord. It makes sense, then, that as these levels are opened, we are in the Lord and the Lord is in us.

—*Divine Love and Wisdom* 240

14 All the things we learn, store away in our memory, and are able to call up from our memory to examine with our intellect are called facts. Properly speaking, they are the elements composing the intellect of our outer, earthly self. It is the same with memorized knowledge, which is likewise stimulated by the beloved pleasures of our will, though in this case the stimulus comes by way of the intellectual side of the mind. Anything that has become part of our will, or something we love, has been incorporated into our life, and this is what triggers our factual knowledge. Our inner self always has a window on the facts we know, and delights in them, so far as they harmonize with our passions. The facts that are fully integrated into our passions and become spontaneous, or natural (so to speak), disappear from our outer memory but remain engraved on our inner memory, from which they are never deleted. That is how facts are incorporated into our life.

—*Secrets of Heaven* 9394:1, 5

15 The intellect comes from the will and reveals the will in a visual form, so to speak, just as faith issues from neighborly love and reveals that love in a form, so to speak. The outward covering of the will, then, is the intellect, and the outward covering of charity is faith. To put the same thing another way, the inner core of the intellect is the will, and the inner core of faith is charity. So advancing from an outward plane to more inward levels means advancing from a faith that belongs to the intellect to a faith that belongs to the will, and therefore from faith to charity.

—*Secrets of Heaven* 3868

16 Goodness accompanied by truth makes its way from the intellectual side of the mind into the voluntary side, and we adopt it as our own. In the first stage, the mind falls into doubt. In the second, reasoning puts the doubt to flight. The third stage is affirmation. The final is action.

—*Secrets of Heaven* 4097

17 Goodness and truth that flow out from the intellect and not at the same time from the will are not good or true, however much they may appear so on the outside. When there is a will for evil, goodness and truth divide rather than unite. When there is any will for goodness, though, they do not divide but unite, even if they are arranged upside-down, because they are the means of our rebirth. So arranged, they serve to regenerate us in the beginning.

—*Secrets of Heaven* 3542

18 Evils cannot be set aside unless they come to light. This does not mean that we have to act out our evils in order to bring them to light but that we need to look carefully not only at our actions but also at our thoughts, at what we would do if it were not for our fear of the laws and of ill repute. We need to look especially at which evils we see as permissible in our spirit and do not regard as sins, for eventually we do them. It is for this self-examination that we have been given discernment, a discernment separate from our volition, so that we can know, discern, and recognize what is good and what is evil. It is also so that we can see what the real nature of our volition is—that is, what we love and what we desire. It is to enable us to see this that our discernment has been given both higher and lower thought processes, both more inward and more outward thought processes. It is so that we can use the higher or more inward thoughts to see what our volition is up to in our lower or outer thoughts.

—*Divine Providence* 278a:2

19 Evil that comes only from our will and accordingly without forethought is evil we incline to by heredity, or perhaps from having already acted on our hereditary inclinations. For this kind of evil we are not blamed unless we have justified it in the intellectual half of our mind. Once we have justified it there, though, it is inscribed on us and becomes our own. Then we are held responsible for it. Nonetheless, we cannot justify this kind of evil in the intellectual half of our mind until we reach adulthood, when we start to think for ourselves and develop our own wisdom. Till then we rely not on ourselves but on our teachers and parents.

—*Secrets of Heaven* 9009:3

20 A person's intellect receives whatever is spiritual, meaning that it is a container for spiritual truth and goodness. Nothing good (no neighborly love) and nothing true (no faith) can be instilled in anyone whose intellect is not at work; no, these entities are instilled in proportion to the workings of one's intellect.

    —*Secrets of Heaven* 6125:2

21 To think with the higher mind is to separate our thoughts from the material realm.

    —*Secrets of Heaven* 9407:4

The intellect is nothing but a subtle awareness of one's inner depths.

    —*Secrets of Heaven* 4622:3

22 The role of the intellect grows and increases from childhood to adulthood and consists in the development of insights on the basis of experience and learning. It also consists in tracing causes from effects, and consequences from a chain of causes. It is the influence of light from heaven that brings about activity in the intellect, so we can each develop real intellectual ability. The ability we receive individually depends on the way we apply it, the way we live, and our native character.

    —*Secrets of Heaven* 6125

23 There are three levels to the contents of the human intellect. The lowest has to do with factual knowledge, the middle with reason, and the highest with understanding. These levels are so clearly distinguished from each other that they never blur. The Lord exerts an influence on our rational thinking through the things we truly understand, and on the data in our memory through our rational thinking, giving life to the senses of sight and hearing. This is true influx; this is the true connection between the soul and the body.

—*Secrets of Heaven* 657

24 Our discernment can accept what is good and what is evil, what is true and what is false, but our essential volition cannot. This must be focused on what is evil or what is good and not on both, because our volition is our essential self. It is where our life's love is. In our discernment, what is good and what is evil are kept apart like an inside and an outside, so we can be inwardly focused on evil and outwardly on good.

—*Divine Providence* 284

25 Anyone can see that intending and not acting when we can is not really intending, and loving and not doing good when we can is not really loving.

—*Heaven and Hell* 475

26 Enlightenment is possible only for people who long to know truth, not for the sake of reputation and glory but for the sake of living by it and putting it to use.

   —*Secrets of Heaven* 6222:3

27 Charity is a union of desires felt by the will and a resulting harmony of thoughts in the intellect, so it is a meeting of minds involving both sides of the mind.

   —*Secrets of Heaven* 3875

28 The reason the wisdom and love within us seem to be two separate things is that our ability to understand can be raised into heaven's light, while our ability to love cannot, except to the extent that we act according to our understanding. So any trace of apparent wisdom that is not united to our love for wisdom relapses into the love with which it is united. This may not be a love for wisdom, and may even be a love for insanity. We are perfectly capable of knowing, from our wisdom, that we ought to do one thing or another, and then of not doing it because we have no love for it. However, to the extent that we do the bidding of our wisdom, from love, we are images of God.

   —*Divine Love and Wisdom* 39

29 Intellectual matters can be compared to constantly varying forms, and matters of will can be compared to harmonies that result from the variation.

—Secrets of Heaven 5147:2

30 Heavenly or angelic peace occurs in us when we are attuned to wisdom because of the union of the good and the true and therefore see ourselves as contented in God.

—Heaven and Hell 288:3

MAY

1 The old self must die before the new self can be conceived.

   —*Secrets of Heaven* 18

2 There are two states that we all inevitably enter into and go through if we are to turn from an earthly person into a spiritual person. The first state is called reformation, the second is called regeneration. The first state is a state of thought that occurs in our intellect; the second state is a state of love that occurs in our will.

   —*True Christianity* 571

3 The whole process of rebirth exists in order for us to receive new life, or rather to receive life at all. It exists in order that from being nonhuman we may become human, or from being dead may become alive.

   —*Secrets of Heaven* 848

4 What does not come of freedom, of voluntary choice or willingness, is in no way pleasing to the Lord.

   —*Secrets of Heaven* 1947:2

5 We ought to force ourselves to do good and speak truth. The secret here is that when we do, the Lord grants us a sense of autonomy that is heavenly in nature.

—*Secrets of Heaven* 1937:3

6 If we could be reformed by force, there would not be a single soul in the universe who would not be saved. The means are countless. But since what is done under compulsion is not wedded to us and therefore does not become part of us, it is absolutely alien to the Lord to force anything on anyone.

—*Secrets of Heaven* 2881

7 In people who are being reborn, the Lord implants the heavenly qualities of love and the spiritual qualities of faith not all at once but gradually. When these qualities turn our rational mind into something that is open to receiving them, we are first reborn—largely through inner struggles in which we win. When this happens, the moment is ripe for us to shed our old self and put on a new one.

—*Secrets of Heaven* 2625:5

8 The goal of rebirth is for us to develop a new inner self and therefore a new soul, or spirit, but our inner self cannot

be remade or reborn unless our outer self is too. Although we are spirits after death, we take with us into the other life aspects of our outer self: earthly emotions, doctrines, facts—in short, all the contents of our outer, earthly memory. These form the groundwork on which our inner depths rest. Whatever priorities determine their arrangement, then, those are the priorities that inner things take on when they flow in, because inner things are modified on the outer plane.

—*Secrets of Heaven* 3539:2

9 Very few today realize that doing good deeds without seeking repayment contains heavenly happiness. They do not know there is any other kind of happiness than rising to high position, being waited on by others, abounding in riches, and living a life of sensual pleasure. That there is a higher happiness than those, a happiness that touches a person's inner depths, they are profoundly unaware. Nor do they see, therefore, that such happiness is heavenly happiness and that it is the happiness of genuine neighborly love. This characteristic is embedded in a new will that the Lord gives as a gift to people who are being reborn, because the new will is the Lord's in us.

—*Secrets of Heaven* 6392:2

10 A state of understanding does not commence in us till we think for ourselves instead of being guided by a teacher. It is at this time that faith commences, because faith is not our own until we have confirmed our beliefs by means of our own thoughts and ideas. Prior to that, our faith is not ours; it is someone else's faith present in us, because we have believed not in the beliefs themselves but in a person.

—*Secrets of Heaven* 10225:5

11 During the phase called our reformation, we come to mentally see and admit that evil is evil and goodness is good, and make the decision to choose what is good. When we actually try to abstain from evil and do what is good, the phase called our regeneration begins.

—*True Christianity* 587

12 When truth is being incorporated into earthly goodness, it hurts to begin with. It weighs on our conscience and worries us, since we have cravings that spiritual truth fights against. But this initial pain slowly lessens and finally disappears. It is like a sick and feeble body that can be restored to health only by a painful cure; in that state, it has pain at first.

—*Secrets of Heaven* 3471

13 We are never tested until we are capable of contemplating what is good and true and perceiving it on our own terms.

—*Secrets of Heaven* 2280:3

14 Everyone who is being reborn undergoes trying times. Trials are struggles against evil and falsity, and when we are in the thick of them, the Lord exerts his influence on us from within and fights for us. This we can tell by the fact that when we are being tested, deep inside us we stand firm, because if we did not, we would succumb rather than conquer.

—*Secrets of Heaven* 10685

15 One purpose of our trials is to subdue our external qualities and make them obedient to inner qualities.

—*Secrets of Heaven* 857:2

16 All trial carries with it some kind of despair; otherwise it is not a trial. So consolation follows. Anyone who is being tested becomes anxious, and the anxiety causes a state of despair over the outcome. The actual struggle is nothing else.

—*Secrets of Heaven* 1787

17 Anyone who is being tested is unsure of the end. The end is love, and love is what evil spirits and evil demons attack, throwing the end into doubt. The more love the victim has, the more doubt they cast. If the cherished end did not become doubtful, even to the point of despair, there would be no struggle. Certainty about the outcome comes just before victory and is a part of victory.

   —*Secrets of Heaven* 1820

18 People who are regenerating and becoming spiritual usually have tremendous difficulty seeing truth. Good coming from the Lord influences them, but the influence of truth is not as strong. So a parallelism and correspondence exists between the Lord and the goodness in us, but not between the Lord and the truth we know. The main reason is that people regenerating do not know what is good, and even if they did know, they would not believe it at heart. As long as goodness is hard to see, truth is too, since all truth develops out of goodness. To speak more plainly, such people know very dimly if at all that the Lord is goodness itself; that everything having to do with love for him and charity for their neighbor is good; and that everything that affirms and supports these

ideas is true. In fact, they even cherish doubts about it
and are willing to listen to arguments against it.

—*Secrets of Heaven* 2935:2

19 We hover between denial and affirmation during our inward struggles. When we fail, we continue to doubt, and sink into pessimism. When we win, on the other hand, we do still have doubts, but those of us that allow hope to set us on our feet remain optimistic.

—*Secrets of Heaven* 2338

20 When our previous way of life breaks down in times of trouble, we cannot help faltering between truth and falsity after the trouble has passed. Truth belongs to the new life, falsity to the old. Unless the earlier way of life is destroyed and this uncertainty takes hold, spiritual seed cannot possibly be sown in us, since there is no soil for it.

—*Secrets of Heaven* 848

21 Regeneration is exactly like human development. When babies are born, they live in great mental darkness, knowing almost nothing, so at that stage general impressions enter their minds first. By degrees, as specifics are introduced into the general ideas, those ideas grow more distinct, and still more distinct when the specifics acquire even greater detail. In this way, the particular sheds light on the general, allowing a person to see not only that such things exist but also of what quality they are. The case is the same with everyone emerging from spiritual trial.

—*Secrets of Heaven* 848:3

22 After this state comes a second one, the state of being in a partnership with God. In this second state we do basically the same things, but now we do them with God. We no longer need to attribute to God everything good that we intend and do and everything true that we think and say in the same way as we used to, because now this acknowledgment is written on our heart. It is inside everything we do and everything we say.

—*True Christianity* 105

23 In a person reborn, external traits respond to internal values, which is to say that they are obedient to them.

—*Secrets of Heaven* 911

24 Once our earthly self has been reborn, our whole self has been reborn.

—*Secrets of Heaven* 9043

25 Real things—truths—interconnect the same way communities in heaven do, and they correspond to the communities of heaven as well. So far as our inner dimensions are concerned, each of us is a miniature heaven. Realities (or truths) that have not formed connections modeling the interconnection of heaven's communities have not yet come alive. Until they form those connections, heavenly love from the Lord has no suitable means of influencing them. They first receive life when the two models match—when the image of our miniature heaven corresponds to the image of the whole. Before reaching that stage, no one can be called a heavenly person.

—*Secrets of Heaven* 1928

26 Thought saves no one. It is the life we have acquired for ourselves in the world by means of religious knowledge that saves us. This life remains, but any thinking that does not harmonize with our life dies away until it disappears. In heaven people associate with each other on the basis of the way they have lived, never on the basis of thought disconnected from life. Thoughts that are not attached to our life are hypocritical and are categorically rejected.

—*Secrets of Heaven* 2228:2

27 The indications that our sins have been forgiven are as follows: we take pleasure in worshiping God for his sake, in serving our neighbors for their sake, and therefore in doing good for the sake of good and believing truth for the sake of truth.

—*Secrets of Heaven* 9449

28 If we look even to the lowliest creatures on earth, we see an image of the process of regeneration in the miraculous transformation of silkworms, and of many other grubs and caterpillars into nymphs and butterflies, and of other creatures that in time are embellished with wings. In brief, the whole world on every level of existence is full of symbols and emblems of regeneration.

—*True Christianity* 687:3

29 When we have been regenerated, we have a new will and a new intellect.

—*True Christianity* 302

30 We always long to move from nonliberty to liberty, because this is central to our life.

—*Secrets of Heaven* 1947

The Process of Rebirth

31 Rebirth is continual because we start regenerating but never stop. We are constantly being perfected not only while we live in the world, but also in the other life forever. Yet we can never arrive at such perfection that we can be compared to the Deity.

—*Secrets of Heaven* 8326

JUNE

1 The Lord governs everyone, not only in a comprehensive way, but also in the smallest details. He exerts this influence directly from himself and indirectly through the spiritual world too.

—*Secrets of Heaven* 6058

2 Narrowly speaking, we each have a spiritual and natural world inside us. Our inner self is our spiritual world, and our outer self is our natural world.

—*Secrets of Heaven* 2990

3 Spiritual influence, or the influence of the spiritual world on the physical world, is possible, but not the reverse.

—*Secrets of Heaven* 9110

4 A stream of influence progresses from the divine level and continues in order until it comes to rest on the bottom level of the earthly dimension—the worldly and bodily level.

—*Secrets of Heaven* 3304:2

5 Only through humankind is there a descent from the heavens into the world, and an ascent from the world to

the heavens. The brain and its inner depths provide the means of descent and ascent.

—*Secrets of Heaven* 4042

6 We are led by the Lord through an inflow and taught by being enlightened. The reason we are led by the Lord through an inflow is that both the being led and the flowing in are connected to our love and volition. The reason we are taught by the Lord by being enlightened is that being taught and being enlightened are properly connected with our wisdom and discernment.

—*Divine Providence* 165

7 Inflow happens by means of correspondences, and cannot happen as a result of continuity.

—*Divine Love and Wisdom* 88

8 A vision is a profound revelation received through perception.

—*Secrets of Heaven* 1786

Genuine visions mean the vision or sight of things that really do exist in the other life. They truly are objects that can be seen with the eyes of the spirit, not the eyes of the body. People on earth see them when the Lord activates their inner sight.

—*Secrets of Heaven* 1970

9 There is a general and a particular influence exerted by the Lord through the spiritual world on recipients of that influence in the natural world. The general influence is exerted on recipients that follow the code ordained for them; the particular influence is exerted on recipients that do not. Animals of every kind live by the code ordained by their nature, so a general influence is exerted on them. We human beings, on the other hand, do not live by the code ordained for us or by any law of that code, so a particular influence is exerted on us.

—*Secrets of Heaven* 5850

10 The Lord is present with us through our human freedom, in that freedom, and with that freedom, constantly urging us to receive him but at the same time never removing or taking away our freedom. Therefore you could say that our freedom is where the Lord dwells with us in our soul.

—*True Christianity* 498

11 Something more needs to be said about people who wait for something to flow in. The only people of this kind who actually receive anything are the few who deeply long for it. They occasionally receive a kind of answer through a vivid impression or a subtle voice in their thinking, but rarely through anything obvious. In any case, what they receive leaves them to think and act the way they want to and the way they can. If they act wisely they become wise, and if they act stupidly they become stupid. They are never told what to believe or what to do; otherwise their human rationality and freedom would be destroyed. That is, things are managed so that they act freely and rationally, and to all appearances, autonomously.

　　—*Divine Providence* 321:3

12 Divinity itself cannot teach us and talk with us or even with angels directly, only indirectly through divine truth.

　　—*Secrets of Heaven* 8127

13 Direct influence of truth imparted by the Lord does not provide an actual perception of truth; it provides light that enables the person to understand.

　　—*Secrets of Heaven* 8707

14 The Lord does not force us to accept what flows in from him. Rather, he guides us in our freedom, and so far as we let him, he uses our freedom to guide us to what is good. So the Lord leads us in harmony with our pleasures and also in harmony with our illusions and the assumptions we base on them; but he gradually extracts us. Moreover, it appears to us as though we do it on our own. The Lord does not break our pleasures and illusions, then, since to break them would be to violate our freedom, whereas freedom is a must if we are to be reformed.

—*Secrets of Heaven* 6472:2

15 Ceasing to do wrong is left up to our free will. We then receive an inflow of good from the Lord, which is never absent, because it is present in the very life the Lord gives us. The amount of good we receive with our life, however, depends on the amount of evil that is moved aside.

—*Secrets of Heaven* 9378:2

16 People who want to be enlightened by the Lord must be especially careful not to adopt any religious teaching that fosters evil.

—*Secrets of Heaven* 10640:2

17 People who are to have perception in spiritual matters must have a desire for truth based on goodness and will always be longing to know truth. This sheds light in their intellect, and when their intellect has been enlightened, they are able to perceive something inwardly. People without a desire for truth, on the other hand, know what truth they know from the religious teachings they choose to believe in, and from the fact that a priest, elder, or monk has called it true.

—*Secrets of Heaven* 5937:3

18 Everything we consider true and consequently allowable forms our conscience.

—*Secrets of Heaven* 1002

19 People who have the gift of perception have no need to learn by way of doctrinal formulas what they already know. People who recognize what is good and true on the basis of perception receive that intuition from the Lord by an internal route.

—*Secrets of Heaven* 521

20 When people with perception feel compassion, they know they are being advised by the Lord to help.

—*Secrets of Heaven* 6737

21 There are many spirits today who want to influence not only the thoughts and feelings of people on earth but also our words and deeds, which is to say our bodily level. However, our bodily level is immune to a narrowly targeted influence from spirits and angels, being governed instead by their general influence. When we express our thoughts in speech, and our intentions in action, the process of expressing them or carrying them over into the body follows a set protocol rather than being regulated in a specific way by any spirits. To influence people's bodily level is to possess them.

—*Secrets of Heaven* 5990

22 When we are being reborn—that is, when we have yet to form a bond with the Lord—we move toward that bond by means of truth, or accurate religious concepts. No one can be reborn without learning what religion teaches, and this religious knowledge is the truth that enables us to move toward union.

—*Secrets of Heaven* 2063:3

23 What else is faith but a partnership with God by means of truths that shape our understanding and thought? What else is love but a partnership with God through goodness that shapes our intentions and desires?

—*True Christianity* 369:3

24 The union is reciprocal because no union or partnership between two exists unless each party moves closer to the other. Every partnership in the entirety of heaven, in all the world, and throughout the human form is the result of two parties moving into a closer relationship with each other until both parties intend the same things. This leads to a similarity, harmony, unanimity, and agreement in every detail between the parties.

This is how our soul and our body form a partnership with each other. This is how our spirit forms a partnership with the sensory and motor organs of our body. This is how our heart and our lungs form a partnership. This is how our will and our intellect form a partnership. This is how all our parts and organs form partnerships, both within themselves and with each other. This is how the minds of people who deeply love each other form a partnership. It is an integral part of all love and friendship. Love wants to love and it wants to be loved.

—*True Christianity* 99

25 We cannot be united to the Lord unless we are spiritual; we cannot be spiritual unless we are rational; and we cannot be rational unless we are physically whole. These aspects are like a house, with the body as its foundation, the structure of the house as our rational functioning, and the contents of the house as our spiritual functioning. Living in the house is union with the Lord.

   —*Divine Love and Wisdom* 330

26 When we are united with the Lord, we unite not with his actual, supreme divinity but with his divine humanity. We cannot form any idea at all of the Lord's most sublime divinity, which soars so far above our thoughts that it dies out completely and disappears; but of his divine humanity we are able to form a picture. Our thoughts and feelings bind us to something we have some notion of, not to something we cannot have any notion of.

   —*Secrets of Heaven* 4211:2

27 I have said several times before that heaven or the universal human is divided into countless communities, equaling overall the number of organs and viscera in the body, and that each community relates to one of them.

Although the communities are numerous and varied, they still act as one, just as all the parts of the body do, despite their differences. The communities that belong to the realm of the heart are heavenly ones and stand in the middle, at the core, while those that belong to the realm of the lungs are spiritual and stand around the edges, on the outside. The Lord acts through the heavenly ones on the spiritual, or through the middle on the edges; he moves through the core toward the outside. The reason is that he acts through love, or mercy, which is the source of everything heavenly in his kingdom, and what he acts on through love and mercy is the goodness taught by faith, which is the source of everything spiritual in his kingdom. His inflow brings with it indescribable variety, yet the variety results not from his inflow but from its reception.

—*Secrets of Heaven* 3890

28 Divinity itself, like a sun that radiates all the light there is, causes everything to be seen as immediately present.
—*Secrets of Heaven* 2569

29 The Lord operates through charity, wherever it exists.
—*Secrets of Heaven* 1100

30 People with a perception of the Lord's presence perceive that all events in their life without exception contribute to their welfare. They also perceive that evil does not touch them. So they are tranquil.

—*Secrets of Heaven* 5963

JULY

1 What is spiritual wears what is physical the way we wear clothes.

   —*Soul-Body Interaction* 2:3

2 There is nothing in the physical world that does not correspond to some attribute of the spiritual world.

   —*Secrets of Heaven* 7112

3 The two worlds, the spiritual one and the physical one, are so distinct from each other that they have nothing in common, and still they have been created in such a way that they communicate with each other and are actually united through their correspondences.

   —*Divine Love and Wisdom* 83

4 We cannot think anything without some idea taken from what is knowable by us or perceptible to our senses. What is more, we do not think properly, even about matters of faith and love, until we think in terms of corresponding objects. Corresponding objects are earthly realities, which act as mirrors reflecting spiritual realities.

   —*Secrets of Heaven* 9300:3

5 A corresponding spiritual concept or corresponding symbolic meaning is bound up with the object to which it corresponds. It is like the bond between our eyesight and our eye, or between our hearing and our ear. It is like the bond connecting our thoughts (which are spiritual) with the form of our interiors and through this with the organs of speech. Or it is like the bond connecting our will (which is also spiritual) with the muscle fibers we use when we act. That is the relationship that every corresponding spiritual attribute or symbolic meaning has with the earthly counterpart to which it corresponds.

—*Secrets of Heaven* 7850

6 Bear in mind also that the Lord is everywhere, is in fact omnipresent. Then consider that the Lord cannot make himself manifest to any angel or to us as he really is and as he is in his sun. This is why he makes himself manifest by means of things that can be accepted, doing so as to love in the form of warmth, as to wisdom in the form of light, and as to service in the form of an atmosphere.

—*Divine Love and Wisdom* 299

7 The whole of nature is a theater representing the Lord's kingdom. Divinity is in every part—so much so that there is a representation of eternity and infinity as well. There

is a representation of eternity because plants propagate to eternity, and there is one of infinity because seed multiplies to infinity. These tendencies could never come out in the various members of the plant kingdom unless something divine exerts a constant influence. The influence leads to the tendency, the tendency to a force, and the force to the effect.

—*Secrets of Heaven* 5116:2

8 All representative objects in the physical world relate to the human form, and have a symbolism determined by their relationship to that form.

—*Secrets of Heaven* 10184

9 Our body is a microcosm, since every secret in the physical world is stored in it. Every secret regarding the ether or modified forms of the ether is stored in the eye, and every secret regarding the air is stored in the ear. Whatever invisible elements float and stir in the air are taken into account and sensed in the organ of smell, and those in water or any other liquid, in the organ of taste. Changes of state are actually stored throughout by the sense of touch. Entities that lie still more deeply hidden would be perceived by our inner organs if our lives were in order.

—*Secrets of Heaven* 3702

10 Our individual viscera and parts—the motor and sensory organs—correspond to communities in heaven, each virtually a separate heaven. From these communities (or rather through them) come heavenly and spiritual influences on us, which act on the forms adapted and fitted to them, bringing about effects that we are able to see. The effects seem completely earthly to us, though; they appear under a shape and guise so entirely different that we do not realize they come from heaven.

—*Secrets of Heaven* 3630

11 The workings of the organic substances of the body are physical and the workings of the organic substances of the mind are spiritual. The two act as a unity by means of responsiveness to each other.

—*Divine Providence* 279:7

12 The angels of the deepest heaven correspond to that activity of our body that is governed by the heart and cerebellum.

—*Secrets of Heaven* 9670:2

13 The reason a head stands for the whole of a person's humanity, or the whole person, is that everything in a person descends from the head. It is from the head that the body originally develops, so when we form a thought or intention (which happens in our head), the effect of the thought or intention likewise manifests itself in the body.

—*Secrets of Heaven* 10011

14 On a physical level, spirit means the life imparted by human breath. The breathing of the lungs corresponds to the vital energy of truth, which is the vital energy of faith and so of the intellect, while the beating of the heart corresponds to the vital energy of the will and so of love.

—*Secrets of Heaven* 9818:8

15 The sense of touch in general corresponds with a desire for good; the sense of taste, with a desire to know; the sense of smell, with a desire to perceive; the sense of hearing, with a desire to learn, and with obedience; while the sense of sight corresponds with a desire to have understanding and wisdom.

—*Secrets of Heaven* 4404

16 Inner attributes are each allotted their own region of the face. Those having to do with love belong to the area of the forehead; those having to do with wisdom and understanding, to the area of the eyes; those having to do with perception, to the area of the nostrils; those having to do with verbalization, to the area of the mouth.

—*Secrets of Heaven* 9936

17 A neck symbolizes union and communication between higher and lower planes, so it symbolizes spiritual influence.

—*Secrets of Heaven* 10429

18 Arms symbolize strength and hands symbolize power.

—*Secrets of Heaven* 4934

The feet and the parts adjoining them represent physical elements and everything connected with them. The foot itself and the heel, then, symbolizes the very lowest physical elements.

—*Secrets of Heaven* 2162:2

19 Clothes symbolize truth, because truth acts as a garment for goodness.

—*Secrets of Heaven* 2454:4

20 Three in the Word has the spiritual meaning "being complete and perfect" and also "containing all aspects at once."
　—*True Christianity* 211

21 The symbolism of length is goodness and of width is truth.
　—*Secrets of Heaven* 10179

Corners symbolize strength and firmness.
　—*Secrets of Heaven* 9494

22 The east corresponds to a state of dawning goodness; the west, to a state of goodness in decline; the south corresponds to a state of truth well lit; but the north, to a state of truth in shadow.
　—*Secrets of Heaven* 9648

23 To speak generally, wind instruments express various emotional responses to goodness, and stringed instruments, responses to truth.
　—*Secrets of Heaven* 8337:2

24 Ashes symbolize elements left behind in our outer, earthly memory after their purpose has come to an end, elements that need to be removed so as not to block their replacements, which serve a new purpose.

—*Secrets of Heaven* 9723

25 Why does war mean a fight between truth and falsity, and in a negative sense, a fight of falsity against truth? Because that is exactly what war is in a spiritual sense.

—*Secrets of Heaven* 10455:3

26 Everything sweet in the physical world corresponds to something pleasant and delightful in the spiritual world.

—*Secrets of Heaven* 5620

27 Honey stands for a relatively shallow goodness; and oil, for deep goodness.

—*Secrets of Heaven* 10540:3

28 Heaven, or the sky, symbolizes the inner self.

—*Secrets of Heaven* 16

29 Water symbolizes matters of intellect.

—*Secrets of Heaven* 2161:2

Correspondences

A sea symbolizes facts in general.

　　—*Secrets of Heaven* 9653

30 Gold symbolizes heavenly good, silver symbolizes spiritual truth, bronze earthly good, iron earthly truth, and stones stand for truth gained through the senses.

　　—*Secrets of Heaven* 425

31 Correspondence is all-powerful. In fact, anything that happens on earth in keeping with correspondence prevails in heaven, because correspondence comes from the Deity.

　　—*Secrets of Heaven* 8615:2

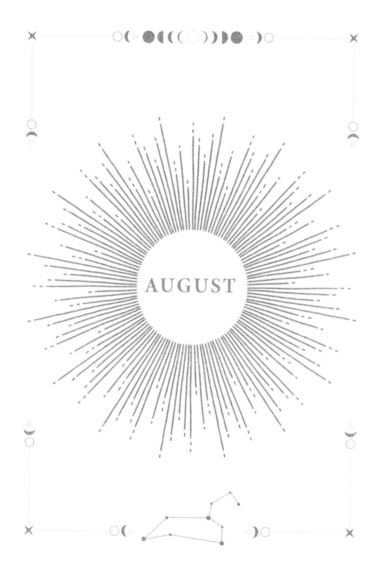

AUGUST

1 In an ordinary sense, a *word* is that which the mouth utters, or speech. Since speech is a thought of the mind uttered in words, a *word* symbolizes the matter being thought about. So in the original language, anything that actually exists and is something is called a *word*. In an exalted sense, a *word* stands for divine truth, because everything that actually exists and is something originates in such truth. All the truth that comes from the Deity is called a *word*.

—*Secrets of Heaven* 9987:1, 4

2 Scripture was written in such a way that the words in it, in sequence, imply a sequence of spiritual concepts invisible to any but those who are knowledgeable about correspondence. It is in correspondence that the divinity of Scripture lies hidden.

—*Secrets of Heaven* 10633

3 Terms or expressions mostly trace the origin of their inner symbolism to the inner self, which mingles with spirits and angels. In every one of us, the spirit, or the actual person that survives the body's death, lives in community with angels and spirits, even though our outer self is unaware of it. Because our inner self lives in community with angels and spirits, along with them it also has access to the universal language and therefore to the origins of words.

—*Secrets of Heaven* 5075:2

4 When we gain access to inward sight (the sight of our spirit), we see the objects of the other world, which could never be presented to the sight of our physical eyes. This is exactly what the visions of the prophets were.

—*Secrets of Heaven* 1619

5 The Word—which was present with God in the beginning, was God, and was that by which everything was created and the world was made—is divine truth.

—*Secrets of Heaven* 9410:5

6 The Word is divine—mainly because everything in it relates not to one nation or one people but to the entire human race as it is, as it was, and as it will be.

—*Secrets of Heaven* 3305:2

7 The Word finds its fullest expression and power in its literal meaning. There are three meanings in the Word answering to the three levels—a heavenly meaning, a spiritual

meaning, and an earthly meaning. Since the Word contains these three meanings by the three vertical levels and their union is through correspondence, the final meaning, the earthly one that we call the literal meaning, is not only the composite, vessel, and foundation of the deeper, corresponding meanings, it is also the Word in its fullest expression and its full power.

—*Divine Love and Wisdom* 221

8 In earliest times, there was no Word. Instead there was direct revelation to the people of the church, and through it, union. When humankind turned aside from the goodness it had possessed, this direct revelation died. It was replaced by another kind. When all this happened, the Lord provided for a Word to be written that would be divine in every last detail, even down to the individual parts of individual words. He made sure it would consist of purely correspondential language.

—*Secrets of Heaven* 10632:3, 4

9 Concerning the Word: In earliest times, when the church was heavenly, there was no Word, because the people of that church had the Word written on their hearts. The Lord taught them directly through heaven what was

good and therefore what was true, enabling them to perceive both concepts from love and charity and to learn both concepts from revelation.

—*Secrets of Heaven* 3432:2

10 The earliest church, which came before the Flood, did not have a written Word but one revealed to all who were in the church. They were heavenly people, so they had a perception of goodness and truth, as do the angels, with whom they also interacted. As a result, they had the Word written on their hearts.

Because they were heavenly and interacted with angels, everything they saw (or sensed in any other way) represented and symbolized the heavenly and spiritual qualities of the Lord's kingdom to them. They did see worldly and earthly objects with their eyes, or perceived them with their other senses, but these were the starting point and means for thoughts about heavenly and spiritual subjects. This ability and no other enabled them to talk with angels, because what exists with angels is heavenly and spiritual, and when it is communicated to people, it is expressed in the kinds of images that are familiar to us in our world. Everything in the world represents and symbolizes something in the heavens.

—*Secrets of Heaven* 2896

11 The representation and symbolism in the Word come from the representations that emerge in the other world. The people of the earliest church, who were heavenly, and who interacted with spirits and angels while they were still alive in this world, acquired them from there. These representations they handed down to their descendants and eventually to a generation that knew little about them except that they had such and such a symbolic meaning. Because they came from earliest times and were used in these descendants' divine worship, though, they treated them reverently and considered them holy.

—*Secrets of Heaven* 2763

12 The inner meaning that sanctifies the Word is heavenly and divine, and it unites heaven with earth; in other words, it unites angelic minds with human ones and in the process unites human minds with the Lord.

—*Secrets of Heaven* 2310:4

13 The inner meaning is not about physical life but about the life of the human soul, or the spiritual life we are destined to live forever. What the Word in its literal meaning does is to depict this life by reference to the substances of bodily life: flesh and blood.

—*Secrets of Heaven* 9127:2

14 There are three categories of ideas that disappear from the Word's literal meaning when it becomes an inner meaning: those relating to time, to space, and to an individual. This is because there is no time or space in the spiritual world. Both qualities are proper to Nature. The reason the spiritual world does not focus on anything limited to individuals is that talk centering on individuals narrows and limits the mind rather than broadening it and removing the limitations. Broadening one's speech and removing limitations from it makes it universal, bringing countless ideas within its embrace and enabling it to express even the inexpressible.

—*Secrets of Heaven* 5253:2

15 Another piece of evidence that the Word is like this and is therefore different from every other piece of literature has to do with symbolism. Not only do the names have symbolic meaning but every word also has a spiritual sense, so that it means something else in heaven than on earth. This symbolism is utterly consistent in both the prophetic and the narrative parts. When these names and words are explained in their heavenly sense, according to their unchanging symbolism throughout the Word, what results is the inner meaning, or the Word as it exists among the angels.

—*Secrets of Heaven* 2311

16 When the Word says, "Your name will be," it means a quality, or "This is what you will be like." Because a name symbolizes a quality, it embraces everything in the person at once.

—*Secrets of Heaven* 2009

The people of the ancient church took God's name to stand collectively for every means of worshiping God and so for every expression of love and faith.

—*Secrets of Heaven* 2724

17 When the focus is on truth the name God is used, and when it is on goodness the name Jehovah is used.

—*Secrets of Heaven* 2826

The Lord's dual name Jesus Christ embraces the same idea. "Jesus" means divine goodness, and "Christ" means divine truth.

—*Secrets of Heaven* 5502

18 To say that salvation is to be found in no name but the Lord's is to say it is found in no other theology—none other than that of mutual love, which is the true theology.

—*Secrets of Heaven* 2009:12

19 It is common for the Word (particularly the prophetic part) to express a single concept twice, changing only the words. Someone who does not know the mystery involved might suppose it to be empty repetition, but that is not the case. One expression relates to goodness; the other, to truth. Since goodness has to do with will and truth has to do with intellect, one expression also relates to the will, and the other, to the intellect.

—*Secrets of Heaven* 5502

20 All the early churches were churches that represented spiritual things in symbolic ways. Their worship was established with rituals and rules that consisted entirely of correspondences. The same was true for all aspects of the church among the children of Israel: their burnt offerings, sacrifices, food offerings, and drink offerings were correspondences down to the last detail. So was the tabernacle and everything in it. So were their feast days—the Feast of Unleavened Bread, the Feast of Tabernacles, and the Feast of First Fruits. So was the priestly role performed by Aaron and the Levites, as well as the clothing of their sacred office.

—*True Christianity* 201

21 The reason being buried means rising again, in an inner sense, is that when the body has died, the soul rises again. When the Word mentions burial, then, angels do not think about the body that is cast off but the soul that rises again. They are immersed in spiritual thinking and therefore in matters relating to life. Everything in the physical world connected with death consequently symbolizes something in the spiritual world relating to life.

—*Secrets of Heaven* 4621

22 "Those who have bathed have no need except to have their feet washed" means that people who have reformed need only to have their earthly dimension cleaned. In other words, they need to have evil and falsity removed from there. The Lord then restructures everything through an inflow of spiritual qualities. Besides, washing other people's feet was a sign of neighborly love, which said, "I will not meditate on your faults."

—*Secrets of Heaven* 3147:8

23 The reason *neatening* means preparing and being filled is that the only thing required of us is to clean house, or in other words, to reject evil cravings and the distorted convictions they spawn. When we do, we are filled with good, because good is constantly flowing in from the Lord. What it flows into is a house (a person) scoured of everything that could block it.

—*Secrets of Heaven* 3142

24 A wilderness symbolizes a state of trial, and the number *forty* symbolizes the length of time it lasts, however long that is.

—*Secrets of Heaven* 6828

When the notion of time is laid aside, there remains the notion of the state that things were in at that time.

—*Secrets of Heaven* 488:3

25 We can train our mind or thoughts on the symbolism if only we believe that the divinity of scriptural narrative is due not just to the story but to something spiritual and divine in the story. If we believed this, we would see that the spiritual, divine component has to do with goodness and truth in the church and in the Lord's kingdom, and on the highest plane, with the Lord himself.

—*Secrets of Heaven* 4989:2

26 When people stay with Scripture's literal meaning alone and do not seek out an inner meaning from other passages in the Word to explain it, they are delusional.

—*Secrets of Heaven* Genesis 22 Preface:1

27 Those who read the Word in order to become wise—that is, to do good and understand truth—receive instruction matched to their goals and desires. The Lord flows into them unawares, enlightening their minds. When they become stuck on a problem, he helps them understand it from other passages.

—*Secrets of Heaven* 3436

28 The inner meaning is not only the sense hidden within the outer meaning but is also the sense that springs from a range of passages in their literal meaning properly compared with each other.

—*Secrets of Heaven* 7233:3

29 There are two dimensions to the inner meaning of the Word: the spiritual and the heavenly. The spiritual dimension is to decipher the inner message as drawn out of the literal meaning (which serves as a springboard for the message, just as objects of sight sometimes serve as springboards for loftier thoughts). The heavenly dimension is to sense only the emotion behind the message of the inner meaning. Spiritual angels focus on the former; heavenly angels, on the latter. When people on earth read the actual text, angels who focus on the latter dimension (the emotion) instantly sense from the feeling alone what the literal meaning involves. From it they form heavenly thoughts for themselves with unending variety, by an indescribable method based on the way the heavenly qualities of love in the emotion follow each other in harmonious order. This description shows what the Lord's Word holds in its inner recesses.

—*Secrets of Heaven* 2275

30 The Lord's Word contains real truth. Its literal meaning, though, contains truth adapted to the comprehension of people whose worship is shallow, while its inner meaning contains truth adapted for people with depth—people whose theology and life are both angelic. The rational minds of the latter consequently brim with so much light that it rivals the brilliance of the stars and sun (Daniel 12:3; Matthew 13:43). This shows how important it is for us to learn about and accept inner truth.

—*Secrets of Heaven* 2531:3

31 The Lord's Word is such that the narratives have their logical sequence and the spiritual contents of the inner meaning have theirs. Our outer self looks at the former; our inner self, at the latter. So the two—the outer self and the inner—correspond to one another, and the Word provides the link. The Word is the union of earth and heaven. So whenever we read the Word reverently, our outer self on earth unites with our inner self in heaven.

—*Secrets of Heaven* 3304:3

SEPTEMBER

1 The grand purpose, or the purpose of all elements of creation, is an eternal union of the Creator with the created universe.

—*Divine Love and Wisdom* 170

2 First, there was a marriage of goodness and truth in the universe and in absolutely everything in it that the Lord created. Second, this marriage was broken up in us after creation. Third, it is a goal of divine providence that what has been broken apart should become a whole and therefore that the marriage of goodness and truth should be restored. Everyone can see on the basis of reason that if there was a marriage of goodness and truth in everything that was created and this marriage was later broken up, the Lord would be constantly working for its restoration. This means that its restoration and therefore the union of the created universe with the Lord by means of us must be a goal of divine providence.

—*Divine Providence* 9

3 All unity is formed out of harmony among many. The way that the many harmonize determines what kind of unity they have. No monolithic unity lasts, only the unity created by harmony.

—*Secrets of Heaven* 457

4 Not one form or part of a form resembles another precisely enough to be substituted for it without some kind of adjustment, however small.
    —*Secrets of Heaven* 3745

Infinite variety could occur only as the result of God the Creator's infinity.
    —*True Christianity* 32

5 In brief, the whole arises from the parts and the parts are sustained by the whole.
    —*Divine Love and Wisdom* 367

6 Everything in us, whether in our outer or inner self, corresponds with the universal human. Nothing ever comes into existence or remains in existence if it lacks correspondence with that human—or in other words, with heaven, or in other words, with the spiritual world—because it has no link with anything prior to itself. So it has no link with the first origin, which is the Lord. Anything unconnected and therefore independent cannot survive for even a moment. Its continued existence results from a link with and dependence on that which brings everything into existence, because survival is perpetual emergence. As a consequence, not only does each

and every thing in a person correspond but each and every thing in the universe does too.

—*Secrets of Heaven* 5377

7 Mutual love and charity bring such people together into one despite the variety among them, because it draws unity out of variety. When everyone practices charity, or loves each other, then no matter how many people there are—even if they number in the hundreds of millions—they share a single goal: the common good, the Lord's kingdom, and the Lord himself. Variety in doctrine and worship are, again, like the variety of senses and organs in the human body, which contribute to the perfection of the whole. When doctrine or worship varies, then the Lord, working by means of charity, affects and acts on each of us in a way uniquely suited to our personality. In this way he fits each and every one of us into the order of things, on earth just as in heaven. Then, as the Lord himself teaches, his will is done on earth as it is in heaven.

—*Secrets of Heaven* 1285:3

8 The essence of love is that what is ours should belong to someone else. Feeling the joy of someone else as joy within ourselves—that is loving.

—*Divine Love and Wisdom* 47

9 Love and charity are the essential ingredients of all theology and worship.

If we took this as a premise, our minds would then be enlightened by vast numbers of passages in the Word that otherwise lie hidden in the murk of false assumptions. In fact, heresy would then vanish. All the churches would join into one, no matter how great the differences in doctrinal teachings derived from this premise or pointing to it, and no matter how great the differences in ritual.

If this were how matters now stood, we would all be ruled by the Lord as a single person. We would be like members and organs of a single body. Then, no matter what our theology or what our outward form of worship, we would each say, "You are my kin; I see that you worship the Lord and that you are a good person."

—*Secrets of Heaven* 2385:4, 5

10 A form is more perfect as its constituents are distinguishably different but still united in some particular way. In support of this, angels have cited the communities in the heavens. Taken all together, these communities make up the form of heaven. They have also cited the angels in each community, saying that the more clearly individual angels are on their own—are therefore free—and love the other members of their community on the basis of their own affection, in apparent freedom, the more perfect is the form of the community.

—*Divine Providence* 4:4

11 The whole of heaven is such that each member is like a focal point for all the others, since each is a focal point for influences coming from all the others by way of heaven's form. This brings the image of heaven out in everyone, causing each individual to resemble heaven—in other words, to be human. Whatever the whole is like, that is what each part is like, because the parts have to resemble the whole in order to belong to it.

—*Secrets of Heaven* 3633

12 Not only does the whole of heaven in general breathe like one person, but individual communities that are in contact with each other breathe together, as do any angels and spirits who are in contact with each other.

—*Secrets of Heaven* 3891

13 All the people in heaven who are engaged in being of service because they enjoy doing it derive from their collective body a wisdom and happiness greater than that of others. As far as they are concerned, being of service means being honest, fair, proper, and faithful in whatever task is appropriate to their station. They say that whenever they do the tasks proper to their station honestly, fairly, properly, and faithfully, the collective body takes on substance and permanence in their good work. This is what it means to be "in the Lord," since everything that flows into them from the Lord has to do with service; and it flows from the members into the collective body and from the collective body into the members. The members there are angels, and the collective body is their community.

—*Divine Love and Wisdom* 431

14 Worship of the Lord actually consists in useful behavior. To be useful while living in the world means to do your job properly whatever your position is, and in this way serve your country, its communities, and your neighbor from the heart; to deal honestly with your companion; and to help others in a prudent way, according to each individual's character.

—*Secrets of Heaven* 7038

15 We have spirits and angels around us, our inner self lives among them, and the Lord governs us through them. As to our inner levels, or as to our thoughts and feelings, we each exist in community with these beings, even though we are unaware of it. Everything we think and will comes from there—so much so that if the communities of spirits and angels in which we exist were taken away from us, we would instantly lose all thought and will. More than that, we would instantly fall down completely dead.

—*Secrets of Heaven* 4067:2

16 Whatever the goodness in us is like, such is the community of angels with us; and whatever the evil in us is like, such is the community of evil spirits with us. We ourselves summon these communities to us, or place ourselves in the company of such beings, because like associates with like. Changes in state are nothing but changes of community.

—*Secrets of Heaven* 4067:3

17 People do not know what the spiritual and earthly planes are, let alone how they differ, what correspondence is, or what inflow is. They do not know that when the spiritual level acts on the organic forms of the body, it enables them to function in a living way, to all appearances; or that without this inflow and correspondence, not even the smallest particle of the body could live or move.

Personal experience has taught me the situation in all this—not only that heaven exerts a general influence, but also that the individual communities exert a specific one.

I have also learned which communities act on this physical organ or that, on this part or that, and what those communities are like. Each organ or part has not one community but many acting on it, and each community has many members. The more there are, the stronger and more perfect the correspondence, because strength and perfection result from a large, like-minded multitude of people joining forces in a heavenly form. So the impetus flowing into each part becomes stronger and more perfect the more people there are.

—*Secrets of Heaven* 3629

18 Just as an earthly love can rise up by levels and become spiritual and heavenly, it can also go down by levels and become sensory and physical. It goes down to the extent that it loves being in control with no love of service, simply for love of ourselves.

—*Divine Love and Wisdom* 424

19 People who live good lives do not condemn anyone with a different opinion but leave it up to that person's beliefs and conscience. They extend the same tolerance even to people outside the church.

—*Secrets of Heaven* 4468

20 When there is a will for evil, goodness and truth divide rather than unite. When there is any will for goodness, though, they do not divide but unite, even if they are arranged upside-down, because they are the means of our rebirth. So arranged, they serve to regenerate us in the beginning.

—*Secrets of Heaven* 3542

21 Mutual love is the foundation of heaven. Heaven itself abides and consists in mutual love, as does all its good fellowship and like-mindedness. Anything in the other world that destroys unity violates the pattern of heaven itself and consequently aims at the destruction of the whole.

—*Secrets of Heaven* 2027

22 A life of neighborly love involves thinking well of people, wanting what is good for them, and feeling personal joy in the notion that others too are saved. If we wish to see no one saved but those who believe as we do, and particularly if we resent any other arrangement, our life is not one of neighborly love.

—*Secrets of Heaven* 2284:5

23 The reason we do not become rational to the highest degree we are capable of is that our love, which is a matter of our intent, cannot be raised up in the same way as our wisdom, which is a matter of our discernment. The love that is a matter of intent is raised only by abstaining from evils as sins and then by those good actions of thoughtfulness that are acts of service, acts that we are then performing from the Lord. So if the love that is a matter of intent is not raised up along with it, then no matter how high the wisdom that is a matter of our discernment has risen, it ultimately falls back to the level of its love.

—*Divine Love and Wisdom* 258

24 When goodness and truth have formed a bond in us, we have a new will and a new intellect, so we have new life. When that is the sort of person we are, there is worship of God in every deed we do. This is because at every point we are then looking to the Deity, revering him, loving him, and consequently worshiping him.

—*Secrets of Heaven* 10143:3

25 The Lord's mercy is universal.
  —*Secrets of Heaven* 2589

26 We are all given the means of salvation, and the nature of heaven is to provide a place there for all who lead good lives, no matter what their religion may be.

—*Divine Providence* 330:4

27 The Lord is omnipresent; and everywhere he is present, he is present with his entire essence. It is impossible for him to take out some of his essence and give part of it to one person and another part to another. He gives it all. He also gives us the ability to adopt as much as we wish of it, whether a little or a lot.

—*True Christianity* 364:3

28 The Lord's church exists with everyone who is in a state that welcomes neighborly love and faith from him. Such an individual is actually a church, and individuals in larger numbers who have the church in them make up a composite church.

—*Secrets of Heaven* 8938

29 The Lord's church is plainly not "here or there" (Luke 17:12) but everywhere where people live by the commandments of neighborly love. That is why the Lord's church lies scattered throughout the globe and yet is one church. When religion consists in life, not in theology separated from life, the church is unified.

—*Secrets of Heaven* 8152

30 The church is an image of heaven, because it is the Lord's kingdom on earth. Heaven is divided into many overall communities and into smaller subgroups, but goodness still unifies them. Religious truth there accords with goodness, because it has goodness as its origin and its goal. If heaven were divided up along the lines of religious truth, not of goodness, it would cease to exist. There would be no unanimity, because the Lord could not give the inhabitants unity of life, or a unified soul. This is possible only where there is goodness, which is to say, where there is love for the Lord and love for one's neighbor. After all, love unites everyone, and when each individual loves what is good and true, it is common ground received from the Lord that unites them all. Therefore it is the Lord himself who does so. Love for goodness and truth is what is called love for one's neighbor, because one's neighbor is a person with goodness and therefore truth. In an abstract sense, one's neighbor is goodness itself and the truth that goes with it.

—*Secrets of Heaven* 4837:3

OCTOBER

1 The death of what we consider during our worldly existence to be the all-in-all of life is when we actually first start to live. The life we then take up is indescribable and unlimited, by comparison, and we are totally unaware of it as long as we are involved in evil.

   —*Secrets of Heaven* 3175:4

2 In anyone who is reforming and becoming spiritual the dead part is buried, so to speak, and a new, living part rises again. So in place of the night in such a person, or in place of the dark and cold, morning dawns with its life and warmth.

   —*Secrets of Heaven* 2955

3 If we abstain from evils as sins and turn to the Lord, the spiritual level is opened, and ultimately the heavenly level. This opening is accomplished by a spiritual life, a life in accord with divine precepts, and that unless we live by those precepts, we remain centered on the physical world.

   —*Divine Love and Wisdom* 248

4 It is an eternal truth that life is not ours; but if it did not seem to be, we would have no life at all.

   —*Secrets of Heaven* 1712:3

5 People have three overall dimensions: the bodily, the earthly, and the rational. The bodily dimension is on the outside, the earthly is in the middle, and the rational is inside. To the extent that one dimension dominates over another in us, we are described as being body-centered, earthly, or rational.

—*Secrets of Heaven* 4038:2

6 The purpose of spiritual crisis is to subdue bodily concerns.

—*Secrets of Heaven* 2819

7 It is generally recognized that we perceive within ourselves the things that our eyes see and our ears hear, that these things more or less pass from the world through our eyes or ears into our thoughts and so into our intellect. If it is something we love, it passes from there into our will and then from our will by way of our intellect into spoken words and physical action. This is the standard cycle from the world through our earthly self into our spiritual self and from there back into the world. It is important, however, to know that the cycle has its inception in the will, which is the inmost core of our life. And if we are intent on what is good, our will is regulated

from heaven by the Lord, even if it seems otherwise. This cycle is the cycle of our rebirth, so it is the cycle of our spiritual life.

—*Secrets of Heaven* 10057:2, 4

8 The last part of a state means when a previous state ends and a new one begins. A new state begins in a person being reborn when things turn upside-down, which happens when inner attributes take control of outer attributes, and outer attributes start to serve inner ones, in the area both of the intellect and of the will. Regenerating people can tell this is happening when something inside them persuades them not to let sensual pleasures and bodily or earthly gratifications reign supreme, dragging intellectual matters onto their side to justify them. At this stage, the previous state is at its end, and a new state is in its beginnings.

—*Secrets of Heaven* 5159

9 We cannot undergo times of trial unless we have a goodness based on truth—that is, unless we have a love or desire for truth. If we do not love or desire truth as we know it, we do not care about it; but if we do love it, we are anxious that it not be harmed. The life of our intellect

consists solely in what we believe to be true, and the life of our will, in what we have convinced ourselves is good. An attack on what we consider true is an attack on the life of our intellect, and an attack on what we are sure is good is an attack on the life of our will. When we are being tested, then, it is our life that is at stake.

—*Secrets of Heaven* 4274

10 We ought to compel ourselves to do good, obey what the Lord has commanded, and speak truly. In so doing we are humbling ourselves under the Lord's hands, or in other words, submitting to the authority of divine goodness and truth. This fact embraces more hidden information than can possibly be explained in a few words.

—*Secrets of Heaven* 1937

11 Trials are the divine means for removing falsity.

—*Secrets of Heaven* 4256

12 Times of trial occur when we are actively regenerating (no one can be reborn without undergoing trial), and they are brought about by the evil spirits around us. At such times we are brought into the state of evil that is ours, or rather the state of evil characterizing the part of us that is most our own. When we enter this state, evil, hellish spirits surround us. When they notice that angels are guarding us from inside, they stir up the distorted thoughts we have had and the wrongs we have done, but the angels defend us from within. This fight is what we perceive as a trial, but so dimly that we can hardly tell it is not simple anxiety. We humans—especially those of us who disbelieve in spiritual inflow—live in a totally obscure state. We sense scarcely a thousandth of the issues over which the evil spirits and angels are fighting. Yet we and our eternal salvation are the whole point, and we provide the resources. What is inside us supplies both the ammunition with which the combatants fight and the issues over which they fight.

I have been allowed to know for certain that this is how the case stands. I have heard the fighting, perceived the inflow, and seen the spirits and angels. I have also spoken with them about the fight during and after it.

—*Secrets of Heaven* 5036:2

13 The primary time for trials to occur is when we are becoming spiritual, because we then understand doctrinal truth in spiritual terms. Often we are unaware that we do, but the angels with us see something spiritual in our earthly preoccupations, because our inner levels then lie open to heaven. That is why we end up among angels after life in the world, if we have been reborn, and there we see and perceive a spiritual dimension that previously seemed earthly to us. If we are this kind of person, angels can defend us when evil spirits attack us during our crises, because they then have a platform on which they can operate. They act on what is spiritual in us, and through what is spiritual on what is earthly.

—*Secrets of Heaven* 5036:3

14 If we believed the way things really are, that everything good comes from God and everything evil from hell, then we would not take credit for the good within us or blame for the evil.

Whenever we thought or did anything good, we would focus on the Lord, and any evil that flowed in we would throw back into the hell it came from.

—*Heaven and Hell* 302

15 The act comes first; our will to do it comes afterward. What we do at the urging of our intellect we eventually do with our will and finally take on as a habit. At that point it is infused into our inner, rational self. Once it has been infused we no longer do what is good from truth but from goodness, because we start to feel a certain bliss and to sense something of heaven in it. This feeling remains with us after death, and through it the Lord lifts us into heaven.

—*Secrets of Heaven* 4353:3

16 The love that is a matter of intent is raised only by abstaining from evils as sins and then by those good activities of thoughtfulness that are acts of service, acts that we are then performing from the Lord.

—*Divine Love and Wisdom* 258

17 It takes wisdom to know what our own aims are. Sometimes our goal seems selfish when it is not, because out of custom and habit we naturally ponder what something means for us at every step. However, if you want to know what your ultimate goal is, simply notice the kind of pleasure you feel when given praise and glory and the kind of pleasure you feel in useful activity apart from personal benefit. If you enjoy the latter, your desire is genuine.

—*Secrets of Heaven* 3796:3

18 At first when we are being reborn, we experience a tranquil state, but as we enter into our new life, we also enter a disquieted state. The evil and falsity we previously absorbed emerge into the open and agitate us. In fact, we eventually suffer trials and harassment inflicted by the Devil's crew, which constantly strives to destroy our new life. Nonetheless there is a state of peace at our center. If there were not, we would not fight. In the struggles we go through, we keep our eye on that state as the goal, and if we did not have it to aim for, we would never have the strength or power to fight. It is also owing to this vision that we conquer. Since it is our goal, it is also the state we enter after our struggles or trials. It is like a state of spring taking over after states of fall and winter. It is like a state of dawn taking over after evening and night.

—*Secrets of Heaven* 3696:2

19 Trial brings with it doubt concerning the Lord's presence and mercy and concerning salvation. The evil spirits then present with us, who bring on the crisis, inspire strong negativity. Good spirits and angels, however, on behalf of the Lord, use every method they can to do away with this doubt, keep hope always alive in us, and eventually reinforce a positive outlook.

—*Secrets of Heaven* 2338

20 The evil spirits who are with us—and through whom we communicate with hell—think of us as nothing more than contemptible slaves. They pour their appetites and delusions into us and so lead us wherever they want.

In contrast, the angels through whom we communicate with heaven consider us sisters and brothers. They instill in us a desire for what is good and true and by this means lead us in freedom, not in the direction they want but in a direction that pleases the Lord.

This shows what each is like, and that it is slavery to be led by the Devil but freedom to be led by the Lord.

—*Secrets of Heaven* 2890

21 The main purpose of devastation and desolation is to shatter the veneer of self-serving dogmatism. Another purpose is to make it possible for people to receive a perception of goodness and truth, which they cannot do until the self-serving dogmatism is softened up, so to speak. A state of distress and grief that intensifies to the point of despair accomplishes just that. We cannot tell precisely what is good, or even what is blissful or happy, without first going through a phase that is not good, blissful, or happy. From the experience we develop a field of sensitivity, and the worse the negative phase has been, the more sensitive we become. The perspectives we form through

actual experience create the field of perception and determine how far it reaches.

—*Secrets of Heaven* 2694:2

22 The issue in spiritual challenges is dominance, or which is going to be in charge—the inner or the outer self, which is to say the spiritual or the earthly self, since they oppose one another. When we are being tested, the Lord governs our inner, spiritual self through angels, and our outer, earthly self through spirits from hell. The struggle between them is what we sense as a crisis.

—*Secrets of Heaven* 3927:3

23 *And took bread and a flask of water* symbolizes what is good and true. The text speaks of a *flask* of water because the amount of truth we are given is very small to start with. Specifically, we are given as much as we can handle at that point, which is what putting it on her shoulder symbolizes. Eventually their water runs out and they then receive help from the Lord.

—*Secrets of Heaven* 2674

24 We can look evil even when we are good inside. That is why no one is ever allowed to judge the quality of another's spiritual life. Again, only the Lord knows this. Everyone, though, is allowed to judge the quality of another's private and public life, since this is a matter of concern to human society.

—*Secrets of Heaven* 2284:3

25 People undergoing this kind of devastation or purging are reduced even to the point of despair, and when they reach that stage, they then accept comfort and help from the Lord. Eventually they are taken from that state to heaven, where among the angels they essentially relearn what there is to know about religious goodness and truth.

—*Secrets of Heaven* 2694:2

26 I have also seen angels scatter some hundreds of thousands of evil spirits and cast them into hell. A vast multitude is powerless against them. The skills and wiles and alliances of evil spirits amount to nothing.

—*Heaven and Hell* 228

27 The situation is that when the earthly self adopts spiritual qualities, everything produced by evil cravings and false convictions—and so everything that disquiets us—goes away. Everything involved in a desire for what is

good and true—and so everything that creates peace—
approaches. All disquiet is the result of evil and falsity,
while all peace is the result of goodness and truth.

—*Secrets of Heaven* 3170

28 Affirmation and acknowledgment are the first general step in a person who is being reborn, but the last in
a person who has been reborn. A person who is being
reborn, you see, starts with affirmation that sacred faith
and goodness of life exist, but a regenerate person, who is
spiritual, possesses real spiritual goodness and therefore
views the affirmation of their existence as coming last.
Such a person has already confirmed the importance of
holiness in faith and goodness in life.

—*Secrets of Heaven* 3923

29 When bodily concerns have been removed, our inner
levels are bathed in light.

—*Secrets of Heaven* 3492

30 Truth comes into its proper light when love comes into
its proper clarity.

—*Secrets of Heaven* 10201:4

31 When our inner self unites with our outer self, day breaks on us, because we then enter a state that is spiritual, or heavenly. We can even see a dawnlike glow, if our state allows us to perceive it. If not, our intellect is at least enlightened, and we seem to ourselves like one who wakes from sleep in the morning, when dawn first brightens and begins the day.

—*Secrets of Heaven* 4283:2

NOVEMBER

1 Every one of our ideas, every one of our feelings, and indeed every shred of feeling in us, no matter how small, is an image and portrait of us. To put it another way, each of these contains an element—whether closely or distantly related—of every thought in our intellect and every impetus of our will.

—*Secrets of Heaven* 803:2

2 Everything good and true comes down from the Lord and goes up to him. In other words, he is the first and the last. Humankind was created so that the Lord's divine qualities could descend through us right to the outermost level of the physical world and climb from the outermost level of the world up to him. In this way humankind would be an intermediary uniting the Divine with the physical world, and the physical world with the Divine. Through humankind as the uniting medium, the very outermost plane of the physical world would be alive with the Divine. This would actually happen, if we lived according to the divine plan.

—*Secrets of Heaven* 3702

3 It is from the core essence of Jehovah, or the Lord, that every human is human and can be called human. The

heavenly trait that makes us human is loving the Lord and loving our neighbor. To love others is to be human, because for one thing, to love them is to be an image of the Lord, and for another, that love is something we receive from the Lord.

—*Secrets of Heaven* 1894

4 A human being is nothing else but an organ or vessel that receives life from the Lord; we do not live on our own. The life that flows into us from the Lord comes from his divine love. This love, or the life that radiates from it, flows in and bestows itself on the vessels in our rational and earthly minds. Such vessels in us face away from the life force because of the evil we inherit by birth and the evil we ourselves acquire by committing it. However, so far as it can do so, the inflowing life repositions the vessels to receive itself.

—*Secrets of Heaven* 3318:2

5 People who are in correspondence—whose outer self harmonizes with their inner self—have a spirit that is radiant and beautiful, as heavenly love is when embodied.

—*Secrets of Heaven* 3425:3

6 Even if the human population grew indefinitely, no one would have the same face as another. No one would have the same inner face, that is, the same personality as another, or even same voice. This variation is even more unbounded when it comes to truth and goodness, which belong to the spiritual world. This boundlessness of everything in the spiritual world and in the physical world as well is due to the fact that it all emerges from what is infinite. The endlessness that exists in both worlds therefore shows plainly that divinity is infinite.

—*Secrets of Heaven* 6232:3, 4

7 In the spiritual world one individual is present to another if only that presence is intensely desired. This is because one person sees another in thought in this way and identifies with that individual's state.

—*Heaven and Hell* 194

8 When people who are several hundred or several thousand miles apart appear before the inner senses, they can be so close (depending on their spiritual location) that they sometimes touch. As a result, if several people were to have their inner eyes opened on earth, they could

congregate and talk together, even if one were in India and another in Europe.

—*Secrets of Heaven* 1277

9 I was shown what the form of heaven is like in its lowest realm; it resembled the pattern of folds seen in human brains. A perceptible view of its flow or circular motion was granted to me, the demonstration lasting several days.

From this experience I could tell that the form of the brain matches the pattern of movement in heaven. The deeper parts of the brain, invisible to the eye, match the deeper structures of heaven, which are totally incomprehensible. The angels said this shows that we were created to reflect the structure of the three heavens. So the image of heaven is imprinted on us in such a perfect way that we are a miniature heaven at its smallest scale, which is why we have a correspondence with the heavens.

—*Secrets of Heaven* 4041

10 There are two things that seem indispensable to us while we are living in the world, because they are hallmarks of our nature. Those two are space and time. To live in space and time, then, is to live in the world—the physical world. Both disappear in the other life. Instead they have states. States in the next life correspond to space and time in the physical world. A state of being corresponds to space, and a state of emergence, to time.

—*Secrets of Heaven* 2625

11 Neither time and the passage of time nor space and extension in space can be used to describe our inner depths, or our feelings and the thoughts they produce. They do not exist in time or in a place, even though they seem to do so, as far as our worldly senses can tell. Rather they exist in inner dimensions corresponding to time and place. These corresponding dimensions can only be called states; there is no other word for them.

—*Secrets of Heaven* 4850

12 The emotions involved in real love draw us out of our bodily and worldly concerns, lifting our mind toward heaven and freeing us from the restraints of time. Time is an appearance we fall into when we reflect on things we do not feel moved by or love—in other words, things that are tedious.

When we are in a state of heavenly love or emotion, we are in an angelic state. We seem to step outside of time if there is no impatience in our mood. Impatience is a bodily emotion, and the more we succumb to it, the more we are trapped in time.

—*Secrets of Heaven* 3827

13 All of our freedom has our life at its center, because it has our love at its center. Whatever we do out of love seems free to us. Heavenly love is present within that freedom when we force ourselves to resist evil and falsity and to do good. At such a time, heavenly love is what the Lord introduces into us and uses to create a sense of autonomy in us. As a result, the Lord wants it to appear to us as if we have true self-determination, even though we do not. In the other world, the Lord takes this autonomy that we have acquired through apparent self-compulsion during the life of the body and fills it full of pleasure and happiness without limit. We also receive greater and greater enlightenment. In fact, we come to believe firmly in the truth of the idea that we have not really compelled ourselves at all, but that even the very smallest efforts of our will came from the Lord. It becomes clear to us that the purpose of our apparent independence was to enable us to receive a new will from the Lord as our own and in this way adopt a life of heavenly love. The Lord wants to share what is his—and therefore what is heavenly—with every single person. He wants it to feel as if it belongs to us and resides in us, even though it does not. Angels have this sense of ownership. The more sure they are of the truth that everything good and true comes from the Lord, the more pleasure and happiness they gain from this sense of ownership.

—*Secrets of Heaven* 1937:6

14 We are all distinguished from each other in the next life according to our type of freedom. To put the same thing another way, we are distinguished according to what we love and desire. Consequently, we are distinguished according to the pleasures of our life, which is the same as saying we are distinguished according to our life.

—*Secrets of Heaven* 2873

15 No one receives comfort from anything but what she or he loves.

—*Secrets of Heaven* 2841

16 When we gain our most profound joy, we are in our own heavenly joy; we cannot bear any deeper variety, which would only end up turning painful for us.

—*Secrets of Heaven* 543

17 The inmost recesses are where heavenly joy comes from.
—Secrets of Heaven 545

18 Because angels love the Lord and share in that love with others, they also possess all truth. As a result they possess all wisdom and understanding, covering not only heavenly and spiritual subjects but also rational and earthly ones. Love puts angels at the actual origins or source of these things; that is, it makes angels aware of purposes and causes. Love does this, because the Lord does it. To see a thing in terms of its origins, or in terms of its purposes and causes, is to look from heaven at everything below, even on earth.

—Secrets of Heaven 2572:3

19 The purpose makes the person, and the nature of the purpose determines the nature of the person and therefore the nature of the person's humanity after death.

—Secrets of Heaven 4054:2

20 The very purpose we love circumscribes our life and distinguishes us from others.

—Secrets of Heaven 4459:7

21 This shows why our purpose determines our happiness or unhappiness in the next life. The purpose is the core of every cause. In fact, if the purpose is not present in the cause—is not the all-in-all of the cause—it is not a cause. The purpose is likewise the core of every effect, because the effect stems from a purpose-dependent cause. As a result, everything we have in us draws its existence from our purpose. So in the other world we live in a state that mirrors the state of our purpose.

—*Secrets of Heaven* 3562

22 The purposes we have are actually the different kinds of love we feel, because what we love, we hold as our purpose. And since the things we love constitute the core of our life, so do our goals.

—*Secrets of Heaven* 3570:3

23 If you take the love away, there is no longer any intention, so there is no action.

—*Divine Providence* 3

24 The reason the aim determines whether a desire is real, feigned, or deceitful is that our purpose is our very life.

What we live for—in other words, what we love—is what we hold as our goal. When the welfare of our neighbor, the larger community, the church, and the Lord's kingdom forms our goal, our soul dwells in the Lord's kingdom and therefore in the Lord. The Lord's kingdom is nothing other than a kingdom of purposes and usefulness seeking the good of the whole human race. Even the angels who attend us concern themselves only with our goals. So far as our ultimate goal matches that of the Lord's kingdom, the angels delight in us and bind themselves to us as their sisters or brothers. So far as we make ourselves the ultimate goal, though, the angels withdraw and evil spirits from hell move closer. The people in hell have no other goal.

—*Secrets of Heaven* 3796:4

25 The soul should be our purpose. Except that the soul should not be a final, but only an intermediate purpose. We should take care of our soul not for its own sake, but for the sake of services we then perform in both worlds. And when being useful is our goal, the Lord is our goal. Having something for a purpose means loving it above all else.

—*Secrets of Heaven* 5949:2, 3

26 Knowledge must have usefulness as its goal. When it has usefulness as its goal, it has life as its goal, since life has everything to do with being useful, because it has everything to do with purpose. If we do not acquire knowledge for the sake of a useful life, the knowledge lacks any importance, because it lacks usefulness.

—Secrets of Heaven 1964:2

27 In love for our fellow humans there is life, but never in truth without that love.

—Secrets of Heaven 1928:2

28 Love has service as its goal.

—Divine Love and Wisdom 297

29 Before the organic forms of the body came into being, their purpose existed, and this purpose brought those forms into being and adapted them to itself, rather than the other way around. It looks as though the forms or organs precede their purpose, but they do not.

—Secrets of Heaven 4223

30 The brain, like heaven, exists in an environment of purpose, useful purpose. Anything that flows in from the

Lord embraces as its aim the salvation of the human race. This is the goal that reigns supreme in heaven and therefore in the brain as well. After all, the brain, where the human mind resides, has a goal for the body—that the body serve the soul, enabling the soul to be happy forever.

—*Secrets of Heaven* 4054

DECEMBER

1 The spiritual world is right where we are, not distanced from us in the least. In short, as far as the deeper levels of our minds are concerned we are all in that world, surrounded by angels and spirits there. We think because of the light of that world and love because of its warmth.

—*Divine Love and Wisdom* 92

2 Heaven is not in any set, specific place, so it is not on high, as most people believe. No, heaven is where the Deity is. So it is present with and within everyone who has neighborly love and faith. Neighborly love and faith are heaven, because they are from the Deity and provide a dwelling place for angels.

—*Secrets of Heaven* 8931:2

3 Regarding the soul, which is said to live on after death: it is nothing but the real person, who lives inside the body, or in other words the inner self, which operates in the world through the body and enables the body to live.

—*Secrets of Heaven* 6054

4 Our spirit appears in human form in the next life, just as it did in the world.

—*Secrets of Heaven* 10594

The body of every spirit and angel is an outward form of her or his love that is completely responsive to the inner form that is the character and mind of that spirit or angel.

—*Heaven and Hell* 363

5 Separation or death occurs when the body either by disease or by trauma reaches a state when it can no longer act in concert with its spirit. In this way, the correspondence ceases; and when the correspondence ceases, so does the union. This is not when the breathing alone stops, but when the heartbeat stops, since as long as the heart is working, love is still there with its vital warmth, maintaining life.

—*Divine Love and Wisdom* 390

6 Our life awaits each of us after death—not our public life, which lay on the surface, visible to the world, but our spiritual life, which lay inside, invisible to the world.

—*Secrets of Heaven* 7032:3

7 Our life awaits each of us after death, not our theology, or at least no more of it than partakes of our life.

—*Secrets of Heaven* 5351:3

8 In an inner sense, old age does not mean old age, because our inner self or spirit does not know what old age is. As our body, or outer self, ages, we pass on to a new stage of life. Our spirit improves with age while our body deteriorates, and it improves even more in the other world. The Lord is constantly leading the inhabitants of that world who are in heaven to a better life and eventually to the bloom of young adulthood—even those who died at a good old age. This shows that on an inner plane, old age symbolizes life.

  —*Secrets of Heaven* 4676

9 In the spiritual world where we all arrive after death, no one asks what our faith has been or what our beliefs have been, only what our life has been, whether we are one kind of person or another. They know that the quality of our faith and the quality of our beliefs depend on the quality of our life, because life constructs a belief system for itself and constructs a faith for itself.

  —*Divine Providence* 101

10 The only relationships and kinships and friendships in the other life are spiritual ones, and are therefore matters of love and faith.

  —*Heaven and Hell* 46

11 Few of us go right to heaven when we arrive in the next life. Instead we spend some time below heaven being wiped clean of the taints left by earthly and bodily types of love, brought with us from the world.

—*Secrets of Heaven* 8029

12 We each take the memory of all our deeds with us into the other life, so we take the book of our life. However, the Lord alone and no one else can judge us all by our actions. This is because everything we do proceeds from final causes that lie deeply hidden inside. It is by those causes that we are judged. They are known to no one but the Lord, so he alone has the right to judge.

—*Secrets of Heaven* 8620:2

13 We are not born with actual evils but only with a tendency toward them. We may have a greater or a lesser tendency to a specific evil. Therefore after death no one is judged on the basis of his or her inherited evil; we are judged only on the basis of our actual evils, the evils we ourselves have committed.

—*True Christianity* 521

14 If we think about something without putting it into act— especially if we think about it without any desire to act—it lies entirely outside us and blows away like straw scattered by a puff of wind. In the other world, too, it scatters away.

—*Secrets of Heaven* 4884:2

15 When people go to the other world, external shackles no longer hamper them, because such shackles are then removed from them so that each individual's nature can reveal itself.

—*Secrets of Heaven* 6907:2

16 Because the upright, when they go to the next life, at first return to the life they had in this world and so to what they loved and relished during that life, they cannot associate with angels yet, not even in their breathing. First they have to be prepared. In the course of preparation they are introduced to angelic life through synchronized breathing, during which they come to enjoy inner perceptions and heavenly freedom. This usually happens in company or in choruses, in which each individual resembles the next in respiration, perception, and freedom of action. I was shown how this was done, again through firsthand experience.

—*Secrets of Heaven* 3894b

17 There are two things that seem indispensable to us while we are living in the world, because they are hallmarks of our nature. Those two are space and time. To live in space and time, then, is to live in the world—the physical world. Both disappear in the other life. In the world of spirits they still seem to exist, because spirits recently released from their bodies bring with them a mental image of earthly phenomena, but eventually they realize that no space or time exists there. Instead they have states. States in the next life correspond to space and time in the physical world.

—*Secrets of Heaven* 2625

18 Because there is no physical space in the spiritual world—there is only apparent space—an angel or a spirit can be visibly present with another in a moment, provided she or he comes into the same state of love and thought as that other, since love and thought create the appearance of space.

—*True Christianity* 64

19 Angels have in their present both past and future. For this reason, they do not worry about events that are yet to come. They never think about death but only about life.

Thus for them, every present moment contains the Lord's eternity and infinity.

—*Secrets of Heaven* 1382

20 There are so many heavens, which the Word refers to as *homes* (John 14:2). The individuals there are each in their element when they are in their heaven and come under the influence of heaven as a whole. Everyone there is a focal point for the influence of all and is therefore in perfect balance. This balance reflects the miraculous form of heaven, produced by the Lord alone, so it comes in every variety.

—*Secrets of Heaven* 4225:3

21 In heaven, I have seen people who had subscribed to nontruth and even to falsity, and this includes both Christians and non-Christians. The reason was that although they had held to nontruth in their theology, they had exhibited goodness in their lives.

—*Secrets of Heaven* 9192:2, 3

22 Heaven's inhabitants do not command or order anyone but communicate their thinking, and the other person acts on the thought voluntarily. To communicate one's thoughts, while wanting the other person to wish for something specific to happen, is influence. On the part of the person receiving the message, it is perception. In heaven their words contain no hint of command over another. No, everyone wants to help and to serve others. This shows what form of government exists in the heavens.

—*Secrets of Heaven* 5732:1, 2

23 All the inhabitants of heaven are led by means of goodness, because such leading is in accord with the divine plan. Everything they think and do therefore flows spontaneously and freely. The case would be entirely different if they based their thoughts and deeds on truth, because they would then wonder whether they should act in such-and-such a way or not, which would bog them down in minutiae.

—*Secrets of Heaven* 8516:3

24 The whole of heaven and its individual inhabitants without exception trace their origin to the Lord alone, in general and in the smallest particulars. This is the source of order, of unity, of mutual love, and of happiness, because this is what causes individuals to look to the health and happiness of all, and all to that of every individual.

—*Secrets of Heaven* 551

25 Angels engaged in similar activities form a single community. There is an infinite variety of good activities in heaven, and each individual is, so to speak, his or her own activity.

—*Heaven and Hell* 41

26 There is a communication of everyone in heaven with each individual and of each individual with everyone.

—*Heaven and Hell* 49

27 The Lord denies heaven to no one. What makes it impossible for people to be in heaven is rather their life force and the communication of this life force, sensed there the way a smell is sensed on earth by people exposed to it. The evil of their life tortures such people more in heaven than in the deepest hell.

—*Secrets of Heaven* 6353:2

28 According to the pattern that everything in the next life follows, evil actually punishes itself, as does falsity, so that evil and falsity carry their own punishment.

—*Secrets of Heaven* 1011

29 There was a numerous crowd of spirits around me that sounded like a sort of chaotic stream. The spirits complained that everything was now going to ruin, because everything seemed disconnected among them, which made them fearful that the end was coming. They thought there would be total destruction, as is usual in these situations.

In their midst, though, I picked up a sound that was gentle, angelic, and sweet, containing only what was orderly. Angelic choirs were on the inside, and the confused crowd of spirits was on the outside. The angelic stream lasted a long time. I was told that it represented the way the Lord works from what is peaceful in the middle to control what is messy and uncontrolled on the outside. Through this core of peace he reduces the chaos on the outer bounds to order, rescuing each part from its natural error.

—*Secrets of Heaven* 5396

30 I can assert positively that spirits are much better at seeing than are people in their bodies, and at hearing, smelling (which must come as a surprise), and particularly feeling, since they do see, hear, and touch each other. This is a conclusion that anyone who believes in life after death would reach by considering that life cannot exist without sensation and that quality of life depends on quality of

sensation. In fact, intellect is nothing but a subtle awareness of one's inner depths, and the higher levels of intellect are an awareness of spiritual matters. As a result, the
capacities of the intellect and of its perceptions are called
inner senses.

—*Secrets of Heaven* 4622:3

31 Heaven's union with us and our union with it are of such
a nature that each relies on the other.

—*Heaven and Hell* 301

ABOUT
EMANUEL SWEDENBORG

EMANUEL SWEDENBORG (1688–1772) was born Emanuel Swedberg (or Svedberg) in Stockholm, Sweden, on January 29, 1688 (Julian calendar). He was the third of the nine children of Jesper Swedberg (1653–1735) and Sara Behm (1666–1696). At the age of eight, he lost his mother. After the death of his only older brother ten days later, he became the oldest living son. In 1697, his father married Sara Bergia (1666–1720), who developed a great affection for Emanuel and left him a significant inheritance. His father, a Lutheran clergyman, later became a celebrated and controversial bishop whose diocese included the Swedish churches in Pennsylvania and in London, England.

After studying at the University of Uppsala (1699–1709), Emanuel journeyed to England, Holland, France, and Germany (1710–1715) to study and work with leading scientists in Western Europe. Upon his return, he apprenticed as an engineer under the brilliant Swedish inventor Christopher Polhem (1661–1751). Emanuel gained favor with Sweden's King Charles XII (1682–1718), who gave him a salaried position as an overseer of Sweden's mining industry (1716–1747). Although he was engaged, he never married.

After the death of Charles XII, Emanuel was ennobled by Queen Ulrika Eleonora (1688–1741), and his last name was changed to Swedenborg (or Svedenborg). This change in status gave him a seat in the Swedish House of Nobles, where he remained an active participant in the Swedish government throughout his life.

As a member of the Royal Swedish Academy of Sciences, Emanuel devoted himself to scientific studies and philosophical reflections that culminated in a number of publications, most notably a comprehensive three-volume work on mineralogy (1734) that brought him recognition across Europe. After 1734, he redirected his research and publishing to a study of anatomy in search of the interface between the soul and body. He made several significant discoveries in physiology.

During a transitional phase from 1743 to 1745, Emanuel shifted his main focus from science and philosophy to theology. Throughout the rest of his life, he maintained